YOUR ROLE
IN TASK FORCE
MANAGEMENT

THOMAS L. QUICK

YOUR ROLE IN TASK FORCE MANAGEMENT

The Dynamics of Corporate Change

DOUBLEDAY & COMPANY, INC.   GARDEN CITY, NEW YORK
1972

Grateful acknowledgment is made to Robert B. Morton for permission to include Organization Development Laboratory materials.

CONTENTS

vi   Contents

TO LAURA

YOUR ROLE
IN TASK FORCE
MANAGEMENT

ONE

THE INEFFECTIVE ORGANIZATION

Not long ago, a firm that designs incentive campaigns for employees prepared a new sales presentation for prospective clients. The presentation utilized Department of Labor statistics purportedly showing that the average employee works at only 70 percent effectiveness. Thus, for every dollar an employer pays in compensation and fringe benefits, he can expect to receive about seventy cents in work done. After hitting the prospect over the head with this disparity, the salesman went on to suggest that, if the prospect were to engage the incentive firm's services, he could reasonably expect to increase the average employee's productivity by 5 percent, perhaps even 10 percent. Even a 5 percent improvement would not only return the employer's investment but provide a profit as well.

But the sales campaign based on the new presentation was a failure. It wasn't that prospective clients doubted that incentives would work. The real problem was that too many executives found it hard to believe that employees anywhere were performing *as well as* 70 percent, no matter what the Department of Labor maintained. The seeming naïveté of the sales presentation often distracted the listener's attention and destroyed all chances of a sale before the real selling could begin.

How effectively do most employees work? It isn't at all uncommon to hear executives argue that their employees (generally defined as most people who are below the executives' own echelons) work at a rate of between 50 percent and 60 percent. Some executives use engineering methods to arrive at this figure. Others try to assess employee capability vs. actual output. And still others say they have a "feel" for what could be achieved were ideal conditions to exist. Whatever the criteria, the fact is that most business executives share this widespread conviction that employee productivity is distressingly low. (Ironically, many employees whose output is criticized agree, although the employee and the executive often don't agree on who or what is responsible for the ineffectiveness.)

The managerial explanation has traditionally been that people don't work better because they don't really want to. And, goes the argument, if employees work at even 50 percent of what they *could* do, it is a tribute to the managerial controls, without which, presumably, output would be even less. No one ever tries to prove this argument, because it is accepted as self-evident that most people just don't like to work. (At a recent conference of front-line supervisors representing many companies I heard the question asked, "How many of your employees do you believe would rather work than do nothing?" There was little dissent when one supervisor answered, "About 10 percent.")

The late psychologist Douglas McGregor of MIT summed up these traditional assumptions about people and how they regard work this way:

* The average human being has an inherent dislike of work and will avoid it if he can.
* Because of this human characteristic of dislike of work, most people must be coerced, controlled, directed, or threatened with punishment to get them to put forth adequate effort toward the achievement of organizational objectives.
* The average human being prefers to be directed, wishes to avoid responsibility, has relatively little ambition, and wants security above all.

These assumptions about the workingman have become famous under the label that McGregor applied to them: Theory X. He wasn't trying to describe how people actually feel about work, but rather how many managers have always *believed* employees feel about work. McGregor hadn't, of course, stumbled on some hitherto unexplored truth. But the attention given him demonstrates the shock value of printing the assumptions. Much earlier management literature had simply *implied* Theory X, judging by the copious advice offered managers by books and journals to help them set up sufficient controls to see that employees do what managers want them to do—what supposedly the employees would not have done without these controls and sanctions.

THEORY Y—THE NEW REALISM

McGregor's thinking in his 1960 book, *The Human Side of Enterprise*,[1] was widely interpreted as an attack on traditional assumptions about people at work (one reason perhaps today why it is no longer fashionable for managers to publicly *espouse* these assumptions). While McGregor didn't say Theory X is wrong, there can be no doubts about his feeling that these assumptions do not portray reality, in most situations, for most people. The implication is that if you want employees to be more effective, your chances of success are better if your management methods are based, not on Theory X, but on Theory Y, another set of assumptions about people and their attitudes toward work. Here's how McGregor described Theory Y:

• The expenditure of physical and mental effort in work is as natural as play or rest.

• External control and the threat of punishment are not the only means for bringing about effort toward organizational objectives. Man will exercise self-direction and self-control in the service of objectives to which he is committed.

• Commitment to objectives is a function of the rewards associated with their achievement.

• The average human being learns, under proper conditions, not only to accept but to seek responsibility.

• The capacity to exercise a relatively high degree of imagination, ingenuity, and creativity in the solution of organizational problems is widely, not narrowly, distributed in the population.

• Under the conditions of modern industrial life, the intellectual potentialities of the average human being are only partially utilized.

McGregor's message to management is quite clear. If I am right, he is saying, Theory Y assumptions are a more realistic view of modern man, and the manager who continues to coerce, drive, and punish those who work for him could be seriously wasting the personnel resources available to him. Ironically, that waste occurs not only because he isn't tapping the mother lode of talent but also because by his autocratic, inflexible leadership he prevents them from doing what they want and are able to do: a good job.

Judging by the response to McGregor's theories, his steadily growing popularity in the dozen years since his book appeared, there are obviously a great many people who believe he is right. Today it is nearly impossible to attend a seminar on management, pick up a management journal, or read a book on organization and business leadership, without seeing a reprise of Theory Y. This widespread acceptance of McGregor cannot be attributed to the overwhelming evidence he presented in favor of his theories, because McGregor didn't present any such evidence. For the most part, his book is a thoughtful essay. By his own admission, the MIT psychologist was not a laboratory scientist.

A TOLERANCE FOR AMBIGUITY

Much of the acceptance of McGregor by managers is undoubtedly on an emotional and subjective level. The man who feels that he is not given as much responsibility as he can handle, that the opportunities for him to innovate are limited, that he needs little external control in order to function effectively in the organization, is the man who finds it easy to give credence to McGregor's Theory Y. A respected colleague, with twenty-five years in the management education field, once told me that most managers she has known tend to look at themselves, their peers, their bosses, through Theory Y glasses, while they hold Theory X views of those who work on lower levels. (Recently I listened to a well-known management consultant describe his efforts to persuade middle-level managers in a large corporation to give more freedom and authority to their subordinates, efforts that failed decisively. Yet, a short time after, he sat in on meetings in which these same managers argued that the executives for whom they worked should give *them* more freedom and authority.)

I have heard it said that the manager of tomorrow will have to develop the ability to live with ambiguity. Culturally, our tolerance for ambiguity is supposed to be very low. Our puritanical heritage militates against it. However, the evidence points to the probability that today's manager is not *that* uncomfortable existing with two cultures, two value systems. One he accepts intellectually, the other, emotionally; one he holds in theory, the other, he practices; through one he views himself, through the other, people who work with him.

Periodically, The Research Institute of America, which offers business advisory and management education programs, surveys managers to find out what problems are uppermost in their minds. For several years, responses to these surveys have shown that large numbers of managers are preoccupied (in an upward direction) with how to get their managers to accept change, change presumably that is favorable to the subordinate manager. The respondents often ask how they can convince the boss to let go of more of his authority, to lessen controls that inhibit their freedom, to encourage their innovation and accept their ideas.

But at the same time, in the downward direction, these same managers, according to the surveys, are looking for ways to "motivate" employees to work more effectively. The way their statements are phrased convinces me that they still think of motivation as something one person does *to* another. (Which, of course, is not what McGregor is saying. Motivation comes from within.)

In the same manager, therefore, you can hear the argument that the organization must create more opportunities for him to exercise his talents, his potential; and in the next moment, he asks the question, "How can I get people to do more than they seem now to want to do?" From above, tradition makes it easy for a manager to say, *"They* don't want to"; from below, *"They* won't let me." Looking downward, the plea seems to be for more task-orientation in employees; looking upward, the plea is for less task-interference by higher management (a plea that one can also find expressed frequently by the rank-and-file).

THE DOMINANT CULTURE

The acceptance of, and the admiration for, Douglas McGregor and his statement of Theory Y are evident. But his actual influence in organizations is harder to find. However liberated, humanitarian, and democratic we may see ourselves individually, when we look at our organizations we see quite a different picture: The culture that prevails is still authoritarian. The structure you are likely to find in most corporations is that of a pyramid, with power concentrated at the top, distributed (often carefully rationed) from there downward through a hierarchy of offices representing the various functions of marketing, sales, production, finance, etc. There will be a clear distinction between line management, through which the authority is distributed, and staff, who perform ancillary and support services for the line.

Rank within the organization is important and usually determines the amount of authority possessed by the man who holds it. There are a chairman, a president, vice presidents, middle management, and front-line supervisors. Decision-making authority is vested in a power center that is usually at some distance from those who are responsible for carrying out those decisions (and who often know more about the factors involved in the operation than the decision-makers). Lines of communications are strongest vertically through the organization (chiefly downward). They are weakest horizontally—between functions that are not related through the same management.

Such were the characteristics of the average corporation when I entered the business community nearly twenty years ago. The model remains substantially correct today. My own contacts with hundreds of businesses have made this clear, as have studies made by The Research Institute of America and other analysts of the corporate scene. Indeed, one doesn't have to be a trained observer to note the prevalence of the authoritarian model. It is sufficiently evident in hundreds of corporate and executive profiles appearing each year in magazines and newspapers.

Through the centuries the authoritarian-pyramidal-hierarchical-bureaucratic structure has been the model for state, church, and military. In business, it has existed since the Industrial Revolution. Much of the management literature of the past two decades has presented evidence that it is outdated and ineffective. There is considerable public antipathy by managers to it. There are obvious pressures today to democratize and decentralize it. But the model persists.

Why?

The easiest answer, of course, is that the authoritarian system works. Perhaps we now sense that it does not work as well as we have always believed it to work. But it has a proved record of success, the only model that does. Of course, outside of a few technical industries such as the troubled aerospace business, it is the only model we have experience with.

On an emotional level, many of us reject autocracy. But on an intellectual plane, we can make a good case that an autocratic regime, in government, business, church, whatever, is really the most efficient kind of operation. No matter our political traditions and our success at surviving as a nation, a distrust of democracy is still to be frequently seen in our society. We are too open, too cumbersome, have too few controls. Much of the anticommunism hysteria that has persisted since the late 1940s derives from the belief that the totalitarian communist state is a monolithic structure, far more efficient than our pluralistic, decentralized government apparatus.

Albert Speer, Hitler's Minister of Armaments and War Production, illustrates just how far we in the democracies have been willing to believe in the myth of the superior efficiency of the authoritarian model. The German ball-bearing industry, vital to war production, was subjected to intensive Allied bombing. "At the beginning of April 1944, however," Speer writes, "the attacks on the ball-bearing industry ceased abruptly. Thus, the Allies threw away success when it was already in their hands. Had they continued the attacks of March and April with the same energy, we would quickly have been at our last gasp . . ."

After the war, Speer learned some of the reasons why bombing had been suspended. He continues, "The air staffs assumed that in Hitler's authoritarian state the important factories would be quickly shifted from the imperiled cities. On December 20, 1943, Sir Arthur Harris declared his conviction that 'at this stage of the war the Germans have long since made every possible effort to decentralize the manufacture of so vital a product [as ball bearings].' He considerably overestimated the strengths of the authoritarian system which to the outside observer appeared so tightly knit."[2] Eight months after Sir Arthur's declaration, decentralization hadn't even begun to take place. The rebuilt factories in the same locations were spared further Allied attacks.

THE MAN AT THE TOP

In business, the vaunted efficiency of the authoritarian model continues to be supported by such arguments as these:

• *Decisions are more easily arrived at.* There is no question that when authority resides in the hands of one man, or of a very few, everyone knows where he must go and what he must do to get a decision. Decisions are made faster than by the democratic process. There is less bickering, less obstructionism, partisanship, diplomacy. The facts go up and the word comes down.

• *Communication lines are clearer.* Generally, they go up and down. No matter how diversified are the functions at the broader part of the pyramid, all lines converge at the top. It simplifies communications when there are no perpendicular lines, that is, between departments and functions. And since all coordination is exercised from the top, presumably there is no chance for conflicting signals.

• *The man at the top is in the best position to know what has to be done.* In theory, at least, he has more information than anyone else in the organization. Therefore his decisions are based on more data and take into consideration more of the contingencies than anyone else could foresee.

• *Employees work more effectively in an authoritarian environment because they know the limits of their responsibility.* The wheels turn smoothly because everyone knows what is expected of him and can concentrate his energies on doing just that. Because there is no confusion about who does what, friction and duplication of efforts are reduced. And people really are happier when everything is spelled out for them.

BEHIND THE MASK

But no experienced executive needs to be told that things just don't work that way. Often, decisions are painfully slow because the man at the top is inundated with problems. Many of those problems shouldn't even come to him, but what employee wants to take the responsibility of deciding what the top man feels he should or should not see? So when in doubt, pass it upward.

There are other decision-making problems in an authoritarian structure. For example:

• There is too much room for whim, prejudice, mood to
affect the top man's decisions. In one company, staff managers say of their boss, "The last man to see him has the
most influence on his decision."

• Today there are too many disciplines involved in running a business, and no one man can hope to accumulate
enough knowledge to make the best decision in all areas.

• In a one-man or oligarchic decision-making structure, some implementation often falls between the chairs,
because the decision information and authority to carry it
out are inadequately conveyed—sometimes purposely—
throughout the organization. Those who are involved in
the decision aftermath wait for official word to start action,
and their necessary involvement may not be realized by
those at the top. "There's always someone who doesn't get
the word."

• People near the power center spend much time and
energy in building influence, in politicking, in fending off
others who are trying to increase their standing with the
top man. An extreme example of this occurred recently
in a large corporation based in New York. The president
has promised the four senior vice presidents that he will
recommend one of them as his successor. Although the
corporation has suffered staggering losses in the past three
years, the welfare of the organization has been subordinated to the political intrigues and infighting of the four
executives.

• When a decision is made by the autocratic manager, it
often means that someone's view has won over someone
else's. It also means that the latter's commitment to carry-

ing out the decision is far from total—that is, after the "loser" has exhausted all efforts in getting the decision reversed.

WHAT THEY REALLY WANT

Actually the efficiency myth is easy to maintain because, until recently, we were conditioned to accept the need for authority without question. This respect for authority is deeply ingrained in even younger executives. To act contrary to the dictates of authority was to risk punishment. Ask the Catholic what it meant to marry outside the Church; it was not infrequent for families to declare such "sinners" as unpersons. Recall the almost hysterical reactions to first draft card burnings! And it is tragically silly today to hear that parental permissiveness, a "new" phenomenon, is to blame for riots, drug addiction, venereal disease, resistance to war, and any other social "ill" that desperately calls for an explanation.

Education was one of the worst offenders. I remember a high school classmate complaining quite intelligently about the deficiencies of some of his teachers. His complaint was dismissed by the parental response: "Now, they know what they're doing." It wasn't that his parents really believed all teachers were competent; it was just that children should not be encouraged to question those in charge.

One ingenious sales manager some years back, recognizing this conditioning to accept authority, utilized it in his recruiting and training. His company, a large insurance firm, had made a belated entrance into the group insurance field. The sales manager resisted the temptation to flood the country with group insurance specialists to match the sales population of competitors. Instead he chose to create a small, highly skilled field staff who would achieve a high volume per man at low cost per office. Since many of the field offices would be occupied by one man, the sales manager hired recruits who he thought could operate independently and on their own initiative.

It was traumatic for many of the trainees, arriving at the home office, to learn that they would be in charge of their own training. Each trainee was responsible for his learning schedule, had to arrange orientation sessions with department heads and to decide what job rotation would be necessary. When the sales manager was satisfied with the trainee's progress, he assigned the man to an office.

The casualty rate was heavy during the first weeks of training. Many otherwise qualified candidates simply couldn't stand the pressure of having to direct themselves. Eventually, however, the sales manager succeeded in developing a force of field specialists whose per capita production was the envy of the industry.

You can see this kind of cultural shock in sensitivity training or in a laboratory group, where there is no appointed leader. Many people are conspicuously disturbed by the leadership vacuum, and they will demand that it be filled. Furthermore, they will complain if there is no agenda. An unstructured situation in which the direction must come from within causes many people much distress.

Today an executive may question the authority he has always accepted. He may suspect it, may despise it. But his conditioning is so strong that to abandon the authority will make him even more uncomfortable.

A few years ago the chief executive of a large transportation company retired. A pioneer in the industry, he had guided the company's destiny from its founding. The present top management is working hard to decentralize authority, to create a more democratic atmosphere. But success has been very slow. Despite management's efforts to move away from the authoritarian model, many people in the organization still behave as if the Great Man were still in charge. "That's the environment they want," says the psychologist who has been retained as a consultant. That's the environment they are familiar with, certainly.

THE BUSINESS OF BUREAUCRACY

Peter Drucker argues that "far too much time is spent maintaining hierarchical systems."[3] There is in the business organization, he writes, an "inertia which always pushes for continuing what we are already doing. At least we know—or we think we know—what we are doing. Organization is always in danger of being overwhelmed by yesterday's tasks and being rendered sterile by them."[4]

The reason is that the average corporation is geared to maintenance, not to innovation and growth. A bureaucracy's first concern is to perpetuate itself. And, of course, the very techniques the corporate bureaucrats use to perpetuate the system usually work against the organization's long-range effectiveness. Let's examine some of those techniques and their consequences.

The *reward system* works to perpetuate the pyramid. Managers jealously guard those powers that are their trophies in the long struggle up the ladder. What greater status can an executive enjoy than the right to decide when and with whom he will share his authority?

Ideally, authority should be granted to those who need it to get the job done. When it is used primarily as a reward, it is granted not in recognition of competence or superior performance but rather in recognition of loyalty to organizational (bureaucratic) values, length of service (survival), and visibility. (The manager who quietly does a good job may find promotions coming faster to colleagues who, though not necessarily better performers than he, make more noise.)

An unfortunate result of this rationing of power is that throughout the hierarchy the authority that a manager possesses bears little relationship to responsibility, which tends to remain greater than authority. A manager usually bears responsibility for an operation that requires the cooperation of other departments over which he has no control. For example, a production manager depends on the purchasing department to obtain the proper raw materials he needs when he needs them. A sales manager has a quota that he must fill, and he can only hope that the production department will produce the number of units he must deliver to customers. A classic example is the staff specialist who is charged with the task of introducing a new procedure or system into the line operation; but, of course, *he* has little or no authority to dictate the line managers' acceptance.

The reward system in many corporations also encourages managers to retain a financial differential between levels. It isn't unusual that a wage and salary program will work to keep a talented man inadequately compensated, because to reward him would remove the differential between him and the manager who, for one reason or another—often not performance—outranks him.

It isn't enough that those who have the power know it; everyone else must know also how the power has been distributed. Thus, the *organization chart* shows the relationship of each man to the others. Everyone is in his little box. Businessmen profess to be shocked and disgusted by government bureaucracy, yet these same critics will work hard to preserve highly vertical, compartmentalized hierarchies in their own organizations. A man is encouraged to carve a niche—sometimes to build an empire—for himself, to construct a territory in which he can operate in the confidence that he will not be interfered with. If a man is honored for his specialty, it is very often for what he has accomplished in the past, to a lesser degree for what he promises to do in the future. And the organization reinforces this maintenance.

Self-protection becomes a matter of vital necessity, and the *respect for territory* becomes inordinate. "Don't invade my turf." It is similar to the flag during the American Revolution emblazoned with the snake and the motto, "Don't tread on me." In one company I know, self-protection has become nearly an obsession. Each time a new executive is promoted, he is given only the vaguest description of his function. The mandate handed him is to carve out his own job, even if it means moving into another man's territory. The upper part of this firm's organization chart is a series of little forts.

Recently a salesman in his middle thirties persuaded his company, which deals in marketing services, to transfer him to the professional staff. Never in the company's history had a salesman become a member of the inside group. But after educating himself in the technical side of marketing, after a lengthy selling campaign on his own behalf, after submitting to a probationary period, the man succeeded in making the switch permanent. One of his interests was in working from the inside to help his company achieve more effectiveness in its own marketing efforts.

However, long after he had been accepted by the other professionals, he was *persona non grata* to his former colleagues in the field department. Here was a talented, intelligent man with, for the company, an unusual perspective. Perhaps no one else in the company knew firsthand the problems of marketing the firm's services. Yet top management, obeying the unwritten law of protection, conspired with the sales department to prevent him from making his unique contribution. His knowledge was not only not welcome, but every attempt was made to keep him from applying it for the company's welfare.

In another company, a man was hired for a sales training position. His background included marketing employee benefit plans. He tactfully suggested to his new management that they were not getting the most for their money from their *own* employee benefits plan. He offered, on his own time, to analyze the program and to make recommendations that would have resulted in considerable economies. The chief financial officer persuaded top management to decline his offer.

Whether in fact, in either of the above situations, the employee could have rendered a service is not the point. What is regrettable is that neither management was willing to have him try to do so, because his efforts would have threatened the territory of another.

EFFICIENCY VS. EFFECTIVENESS

When so much energy is expended to strengthen one's own position and keep others from encroaching, the organization pays a heavy price. For one thing, innovation suffers. There's just too much risk involved. If you succeed, your relationship to others will probably change, and you will have to create new boundaries, new walls. It's true, you may enlarge your empire; but, of course, if you fail, you may provide the other fellow with an opportunity to enlarge his. You become extremely vulnerable to attack from without.

Another consequence of compartmentalization is obsolescence. When the corporate emphasis is on doing well what you have been doing all along, there is little reward for acquiring knowledge that may necessitate change that you are unable to make. Furthermore, someone else may regard your efforts to expand your knowledge as an indication that you mean to expand your power.

Besides, in the bureaucratic organization, inputs often count far more than outputs. Efficiency is rated higher than effectiveness. There are managers who are highly efficient, hurrying from office to office, conference to conference. They wallow in procedures. What is important is maintaining the right kind of profile, in being known as a doer (which is quite different from one who gets things *done*).

Decisions suffer also. Information is essential to a sound decision. Yet information is power, not to be surrendered easily. In a compartmentalized structure, decisions made by a department are based on that department's needs and goals, which may or may not be related to the organization's over-all welfare.

A large number of corporate decisions are made sequentially, a costly and time-consuming process. To illustrate, the top management of the QEM Corporation asks its research and development group to come up with a new product that will compete with those already introduced by other firms. R&D studies the competitors' products and then develops its own that is clearly superior, one that reflects the professional expertness of QEM's research staff. When the engineering people, who are responsible for designing production facilities and processes, see the prototype, they protest that the new product, in its present form, would require either a new plant or an expensive modification of the production capability that already exists. Back goes the prototype to R&D so that it can be altered to make its production less disruptive. When the engineering designs reach the production department, however, there is outrage from that department's management, who see that no provision has been made for allocating and training manpower. Furthermore, the sales and finance departments are equally disturbed. The price of the new product would be too high to be competitive. The necessary training for salesmen would be prolonged and would require time taken away from selling other products. And so on—and on.

The lack of collaboration can reach dangerous proportions. In a small company in the New York metropolitan area, the sales manager has trained his salesmen to sell a new product. The specifications they are selling, however, do not match what the engineers and production force are manufacturing. The sales manager knows of the disparity; he believes it is only a matter of time until his influence on top management persuades them to order the product changes he wishes. The thought that, under the aegis of top management, he might sit down and work things out directly with engineering and production is one he won't entertain. It is of utmost importance that he demonstrate the superiority of his power.

Training is a key device used by the bureaucrat to perpetuate the compartmentalized, hierarchical system in which he is so comfortable. Not long ago *The New York Times* printed an interview with the new president of a large, well-known manufacturing company. He related with obvious pride how his predecessor had trained him over a period of eight years for the presidency. "And I," he said, "am training my successor the same way." It's a reasonable assumption that the goals and methodology of all three generations of presidents will be strikingly similar.

One university that provides continuing education for managers periodically schedules a seminar the theme of which is, "What are your training objectives?" At first the idea of managers spending two or three days on such an obvious question is rather silly. But the seminar leaders know that this "obvious question" is infrequently asked. Most corporate training is designed to teach people simply to do better what is already being done. Seldom do training programs try to anticipate the needs of people who are innovating, and even rarer is the training that is designed around the abilities of the people being trained. The classic distinction between what a man is and what he does is reinforced by most training, and the value of what he does is a function of corporate need as perceived by those at the top. The younger people talk of the dehumanization of the corporation, and their point is irrefutable. When human beings are required to fit the slots rather than the other way around, when talents in a man are ignored, when no reference to them can be found in his position, the result is a tragic waste of personnel resources.

Training, incidentally, can also be part of the corporate reward system. A large insurance company in the Northeast sends its managers to various university-sponsored management development programs that last from six weeks to six months. I asked the training director how these managers qualified to take the courses. He told me that recommendations were made by their bosses, then reviewed by top management, who made the decisions. "How often," I asked, "do the managers themselves ask to be sent?" He looked at me in astonishment. "I can't think of an instance," he said.

Far be it for these managers to ask for the status symbol of a management development program. And apparently it is unthinkable that a manager would try to assess his own educational needs.

THE RARITY OF TRUST

Thus far, I have been talking about a model. Chris Argyris, in his book, *Management and Organizational Development*,[5] describes behavior he found in managers of a company the culture of which was based on authoritarian values and Theory X assumptions. There was, for example, much talk among the executives about the desirability of changing behavior—but in others, not in themselves. They did not see themselves as causing the problems which they admitted their company faced.

In the meetings Argyris witnessed, this was the behavior that he observed most frequently:

Owning up to ideas
Conforming to ideas
Concern for ideas
Openness to ideas

However, the ideas expressed, in Argyris's view, often lacked originality. Apparently, the concern for and openness to ideas extended chiefly to those that do not involve innovation and change. Nor did the concern and openness motivate the executives in most cases to "helping others to express ideas." They did not play supportive roles for each other.

How the executives felt—their emotions—was not often expressed. In fact, Argyris notes that trust and concern for feelings were rarely observed behavior. And yet, people do not and cannot exist on an intellectual, ideational plane exclusively. Much of what we say and do is deeply influenced by what we *feel*, yet these executives to a large extent ignored emotional bases of their thinking.

Argyris found that some of the executives he observed acknowledged their belief that to talk openly about frustrations, confusions, and a need for help, shows weakness. I've heard executives express this thinking. And I have seen them build strong barriers to keep emotions from being displayed, in themselves and in others.

Unfortunately, these barriers play a large part in preventing us from working effectively with each other in our organizations. We share so little of ourselves with others that we cannot form the basis for trust, for collaboration, for honesty. Thus, our bureaucratic behavior is predictable: rational, impersonal, safely conforming, self-protective— all of the factors that contribute to the compartmentalized, fragmentated, fortified, structure consistent with the authoritarian model.

Fortunately—or unfortunately, depending on one's perspective—our organizations, for reasons that we'll discuss in Chapter Two, are facing both external and internal pressures that will render the authoritarian model obsolete, unable to deal with the demands being made upon it. Bureaucracy, in the decade ahead, is a "luxury" that businesses will find they cannot afford.

TWO

THE EMERGING CULTURE

"Democracy," wrote Warren Bennis in 1968, *"becomes a functional necessity whenever a social system is competing for survival under conditions of chronic change."*[6] Few executives would have any problem agreeing with Bennis that such conditions exist. In fact, it's not unusual to hear a businessman, usually unwittingly, borrow a premise from Heraclitus in asserting that change seems to be the only constant.

However, among businessmen, there may be some reluctance to accept the other part of Bennis' statement, that democracy is the only way a social system—and that covers business organizations—can survive.

Why democracy?

The very essence of a democratic society is that authority is decentralized: that is, power centers are found throughout the community or organization. Such a distribution of authority is in rough proportion to the *need for* authority. The people who need it to get a job done should have it, and they are more likely to have it in a democratic than in an autocratic society. And, of course, authority can be shifted to meet new problems or to take advantage of new opportunities.

These problems and opportunities can be identified more quickly in a decentralized organization because information flows with considerably fewer obstacles than in an authoritarian structure with its compartments and barriers that force the information to flow upward to a central point (from which it may never return). In a corporation today, the speed and reliability of information, upon which decisions can be based, may make all the difference between profit and loss, the difference being survival as an entity.

In our national history we've seen that the judicious shifting of power and the free flow of information are extremely difficult to achieve unless each member of the community is conscious not only of his responsibility but of his ability to affect other segments of his society. This holds true in a business organization. Everyone, from chairman to the rank-and-file, is a potential thermostat, capable of sensing changes within and outside the corporation. If the individual sees the importance *to him* of responding to a change, a threat, an opportunity, and of alerting other members to it, then the corporation has a good chance of achieving the flexibility that is essential in times of "chronic change."

In an autocracy the myth prevails that the good of all

can be served by one man—or by a few operating as one. But the idea of a repository of all knowledge, like the Renaissance Man, is an absurdity. As cumbersome as it is, the democratic, decentralized model or organization with all of its imbalances and dissent, serves today's business corporation best.

PRESSURE FROM THE TOP

On an academic level, most executives would probably agree. But as I have pointed out, there is an incongruence between condemning bureaucracy in government while fostering it in the corporation, between praising democracy and suspecting its practicability.

Assume for a moment that you were to sponsor the following candidate for a particular corporate position. In addition to the technical knowledge and experience specified for the job, your candidate has the following profile: He:

• uses initiative, constantly looking for opportunities to innovate;

• is motivated by learning situations in which he can expand his knowledge and acquire new skills;

• restlessly seeks as much responsibility as he feels he can handle;

• believes that he can only truly be effective in helping the organization achieve its goals when, in doing so, he can achieve many of his personal objectives;

• values information relating to all functions of the organization, seeks to acquire it and to share it with others;

• is convinced that he is most effective when his relationships with others are positive, helping, and honest.

What executive would turn down your candidate as unsuitable? He'd be rare. But the fact is that most executives, if they were to appraise their corporate climate realistically, *should* turn him down. Such a man would be totally frustrated trying to be himself in the average business bureaucracy.

There is, however, a new and fascinating movement in the American business community that provides compelling evidence that many executives recognize the disparity between what they say they want and the conditions that actually prevail. This movement, which has become known as Organization Development, or more simply as OD, has as its objective the systematic, systemwide change of the corporate climate or culture to permit a more profitable utilization of the organization's human resources.

While the means to achieve this cultural change vary from organization to organization, the goals are very much the same: They are to:

• create an open, problem-solving climate throughout the organization;
• supplement the authority of status with the authority of competence and knowledge;
• locate decision-making and problem-solving responsibilities as close to the information sources as possible;
• maximize collaboration;
• increase the sense of ownership of organizational objectives throughout the work force;
• increase self-control and self-direction for people within the organization;

• build trust among persons and groups through the work force;

• develop a reward system that recognizes both the achievement of the organization's goals and the attainment of an individual's goals.

At this time, there are perhaps less than a thousand corporations in this country with formally established OD departments, although most of these firms are very large and influential. Nevertheless, managers everywhere are beginning to see the increase in pressure from the top to change the structure of the organization, to push decision-making to lower management levels. Our changing markets, new technologies, and competitive conditions have intensified the executive's need to know. There has been an acceleration in the availability of knowledge that, to run a business effectively, an executive must acquire and apply. The man at the top needs help, and he can no longer afford to ignore the vast personnel resources he has at his side.

PRESSURES FROM BELOW

Clearly, in Douglas McGregor's mind, the assumptions in Theory Y are optimistic and humanistic. While Theory X represents a static and somewhat pessimistic view of the nature of man, Theory Y emerges as dynamic and amenable to the changing nature of organizations and individuals.

Anyone who deals with young entrants to the work force has undoubtedly been struck by the optimism and the humanism that McGregor refers to. A different value system is at work among the young than the one their elders accepted.

For one thing, it is a truism—but no less important—that young people today don't bear what author Caroline Bird calls The Invisible Scar—the Depression trauma. Few young people feel the fear or the insecurity. They don't have the gut loyalty, the gratitude to the man who has given them a job. They don't find their dignity in just having steady work, or in doing that work well. Rather, they find self-esteem in doing well that which they can and want to do. That these are well-founded values is demonstrated by the fact that during the recent, prolonged recession, one could sense no deep fear of loss when talking with young employees. Affluence had not created a façade but a true security.

Nor do members of the young work force appreciate the "blessings" of a quarter-century of affluence. Many of them have grown up in "have" families. For them, there is no acceptable rationale for serving an apprenticeship in order to join the "haves" on their own. They feel no drive to break into the "system," as their parents often felt after World War II. They are part of the system, certified members of the affluent society. So whatever it takes to continue to enjoy affluence, that's what the young demand. If responsibility is where the rewards are, then, they say, give us the responsibility, show us the way up. Don't think you can keep us in the lobby or the anteroom while we prove our worth.

If affluence has created pressure, inflation and urban problems have made that pressure quite painful. There was a time young people, in starting out, lived in the inner city, in old neighborhoods, in apartments. The cities have changed, and many people don't care to live in them any longer. They settle in the suburbs. The housing market is such that buying a home today is comparatively expensive and requires more cash than most young people have readily available. The initial expenses of suburban life, plus the competitive forces that push people to larger and costlier status symbols—the newer house, more powerful car, etc.—create a materialism that can be supported only by a rapid rise through the hierarchy to where the higher incomes are.

There are, of course, other forces in the newer generation that cause restlessness, that displace the old-fashioned virtue of loyalty to one's employer. Education is one. With an educational quality and quantity that he believes far superior to what his father enjoyed, the young employee is not content with the low entry job that his father took for granted. He wants to come into the corporation at a higher level and get on a fast track. And if you don't give him what he wants, he'll go somewhere else.

His loyalty is to himself and to his profession. He is part of the "mobilocracy," to borrow a term from psychologist and consultant Eugene E. Jennings, known best perhaps for his book, *The Mobile Manager*.[7] Managers who make it to the top, Jennings says, are those who stay on the move. "Maybe you can't move *up* every two years," the young manager is told, "but you'd better move somewhere." The manager who doesn't move fast laterally or vertically can't learn enough and won't be visible enough. In one meeting I attended recently of young supervisors, the comment was made by one and approved by others present, "So long as my company gives me chances to keep learning, to sharpen my skills, I'll stay. The minute I stop progressing, I leave."

Peter Drucker, a shrewd and knowledgeable observer of the American industrial scene, said recently in an interview, "What the young people are demanding—and they are right—is more responsibility, more challenge, more self-discipline and a more demanding job."[8]

Unfortunately, there aren't in most organizations enough "demanding jobs" and responsibility to satisfy this craving. At the moment there is a lot of dissatisfaction, much moving around from company to company, the proliferation of titles with little or no additional function and authority.

A new culture is beginning to emerge in our business organizations. Some insights into this culture were offered recently by Dean Harold M. Williams of the Graduate School of Business Administration, University of California, Los Angeles. In a speech at an Arden House conference on "Change or Revolution," Dean Williams said:

"The primary future change problems of society and of business will be human problems. And the determinants of social and political change will be changes in attitude rather than tangible, physical changes such as in population level, income level, urban growth, or new products or services. These attitudinal changes, I believe, will include such dimensions as:

"1. Focus on the *quality* of life—on quality over quantity—from the quality of *product* to the quality of our *environment* to the quality of our purposes as individuals and as a society.

"2. Regard for the individual—his dignity, freedom, and self-esteem in relation to his fellow man and to institutions.

"3. Rejection of authoritarianism, coupled with a challenging of established custom and practice, including a continued redefinition of equity and justice, with regard for authority as a resource for accomplishing society's purposes, not an object of respect per se.

"4. Increased impatience with economic hardship and social injustice.

"5. Acceptance of leisure as a legitimate activity.

"6. Growing emphasis on individual and more immediate gratification.

"7. Furtherance of diversity of choice—from products, to where one lives, to where to apply one's productive talents."

THE INTEGRATION OF GOALS

The values championed by today's work force are both attested to, and reinforced by, the work done by certain behavioral scientists in the past two decades centering on people's attitudes toward work and their motivation to work.

Douglas McGregor, whom we've already discussed, owed a large debt to the thinking of the late Abraham H. Maslow, whose *hierarchy of needs* has become one of the most taken-for-granted theories of our time. Human beings are motivated, Maslow said, to satisfy certain needs, ranging upward in broad categories from the physiological to self-actualization. Here is the hierarchy:

Physiological—food, warmth, sex, other bodily needs.
Safety—physical and emotional security from illness and injury.
Love—belongingness, other people, to be part of a group, to give and receive love.
Esteem—self-respect and the respect for others.

Self-actualization or self-fulfillment—realizing one's capabilities, turning his potential into actuality, becoming what one is capable of being.

In Maslow's view, *every man* responds to the first four needs. The notion of hierarchy derives from Maslow's belief that, a lower need is satisfied first (for example, for the most part, the hungry man isn't concerned with safety or love—he works to obtain a steady supply of food).

Self-actualization, however, is more of a growth need than a deficit need, and not everyone feels impelled to satisfy it. But the man who is trying to actualize himself (and he will never do so completely) feels very strong drives, sufficiently so that if he cannot actualize his potential in one context, he will do so in another. The implication in this, of course, is that if an employee cannot actualize himself on the job, he will either leave that job or stay with it while finding actualization opportunities outside the job—politics, art, social life, avocations, etc. Either way, his manager is in trouble.

A few years ago, I listened while a professor of a graduate business school in the Midwest explained his theory of motivation, one aspect of which involved self-actualization. The "theory" demonstrated that, as opportunities to actualize increased off the job, his investment of time and energy in the job decreased in proportion. At one point in the presentation, I expressed my doubt that few business organizations as presently constituted offer such fulfillment opportunities. The professor agreed with me. So I asked the inevitable question, "What does a manager do if he is a self-actualizer, or if one of his employees is?" The professor shrugged. Apparently the manager had better pray that neither he nor an employer feels the need to realize himself.

But, of course, as many management thinkers have pointed out, the very success of our economy will necessitate far-reaching organizational change. Chris Argyris writes, "The people will begin to think increasingly about and seek intensively for new dimensions of personal growth and self-actualization. As these needs become dominant, the frustration will increase because all the traditional organizations of all our institutions are designed to be effective if most of the participants gain minimal self-actualization . . ."[9]

That is, if the hierarchy works as Abe Maslow said it should. Unfortunately for the theory, attempts to develop laboratory evidence to support Maslow have largely been unsuccessful. The needs can be verified, but it can be shown that people concern themselves with the higher needs even before the lower ones are predominantly satisfied: A man may seek esteem without having the love he wants. Or he may seek self-actualization while still awaiting esteem.

Whatever the evidence, self-actualization is an important concept, and I suspect we'll find it all too common for the human being to want to move from potency to act, as the Scholastic philosophers put it. What is especially noteworthy in Maslow is the emphasis on the *individual* and his needs. McGregor shared this emphasis. "The central principle which derives from Theory Y," he wrote, "is that of integration: The creation of conditions such that the members of the organization can achieve their own goals *best* by directing their efforts toward the success of the enterprise."[10] In fact, McGregor felt that the organization that inhibited this integration suffered—as indeed it does.

What does he mean by personal goals? To achieve wealth and fame are obvious. Some others are to:

- lead, have responsibility for something;
- increase knowledge and skill;
- innovate and create;
- do work that one likes;
- do work that benefits others;
- be considered important, esteemed for proficiency;
- do something one can be proud of;
- demonstrate superior skill.

The list could go on and on. But the thrust of Maslow's and McGregor's thinking is toward eliminating the classical distinction between what a man is and what he does. A manager has every reason to concern himself with the *person* of each employee; he must realize that the greatest motivational possibilities exist when the achievement of organizational goals makes it possible for the employee to accomplish his own objectives.

Maslow's thinking has also influenced the work of Frederick Herzberg, known for his two-factor theory of job satisfaction. Herzberg identifies certain "satisfiers." All motivational force derives from their presence. They are: *achievement, recognition of that achievement, the work itself, responsibility, advancement, and growth.* One or more of these factors must be present if a man is to feel satisfaction from his work. If none is present, the man feels no satisfaction, but he does *not* feel dissatisfaction.

There are, in Herzberg's view, other factors which, through being absent from the work scene, can lead to dissatisfaction. Their presence won't contribute to satisfaction (hence, they can't motivate). He calls them hygiene factors: company policy and administration, supervision, working conditions, interpersonal relations, salary, status, job security, etc.

There is, of course, not a total dichotomy. Salary, by itself a hygiene factor, can provide recognition of achievement, a satisfier. Also in business organizations there is more than a little confusion about the role of education—the learning situation. Clearly, the right kind of learning provides growth and progress, both motivators in Herzberg's view.

GIVE HIM MORE CONTROL

So important does Herzberg see the motivation force in the work itself that he advocates job enrichment, increasing the content of a job, giving an employee more growth opportunity, more authority, more control over his work.

Control over one's job is the keystone of Rensis Likert's thinking, derived from the sociopsychological research he conducted as director of the University of Michigan's Institute for Social Research. Likert, often referred to as the father of Participative Management, defines four systems of management in existence today:

1. *Exploitive-authoritative.* This model is autocratic, distinguished by an absence of confidence or trust among the people who comprise it. Punishment is used as a sanction. There is little interaction between organization members, no teamwork. Communication is downward.

2. *Benevolent-authoritative.* Still autocratic but paternalistic—the kind master. Punishment is used, but there

are rewards, too. Management has some concern for employees.

3. *Consultative.* Decisions are not made in *total* disregard of employees' interests. Communications flow upward, too. Employees get involved to some extent. People are consulted when there is a matter to be decided, though they are not necessarily involved in the decision-making process.

4. *Participative-group.* People have confidence and trust in each other and feel free to discuss matters openly. Communications up and down *and* horizontally. Decision-making is decentralized. There is concern for the goals of individuals. Goals are established by group participation. Rewards are used, not punishment.

System 4 is, in Likert's view, clearly the superior management culture. It is a complex system of interlinking groups —the linking-pin concept. The manager of one work group is a member of one or more other work groups.[11]

ORGANIZATION DEVELOPMENT—A CRITIQUE

Running through all the theory and empirical research is the revelation that our business organizations are wasting their personnel resources, are utilizing a pitifully small fraction of what employees have to offer—indeed, want to offer.

I'm not giving undue glory to the research of the behavioral scientists. The work in motivation is primitive. There is as yet no body of scientific knowledge to guide management dogmatically in developing more effective organizations. Key relationships have yet to be established. What effect, for example, does high or low morale have on productivity, if any? What role does job satisfaction play in productivity?

Nevertheless, executives in many organizations, recognizing the exigencies of the marketplace, of new technologies, of the values of and forces operative in the new work force, and the generalizations, such as they are, that can be made from the data generated thus far by research in the behavioral sciences, have begun the search for ways to change the corporate climate. While we may talk of industrial humanism, or the human relations movement, let's not lose sight of the fact that the rationale for changing the organization is to make it more effective—and the chief measurement of that effectiveness at this time is *profit*.

Unfortunately, Organization Development, through which this change is to be accomplished, is an uncertain field, a stumbling effort. There isn't much in the way of data, experience, and expertness as yet. One thing, however, is clear: The authoritarian model does not have the flexibility that is necessary to make effective use of human resources. Peter Drucker puts it this way: "An innovating organization requires a different structure of the relationship between people. It requires a team organization rather than a command organization."[12]

The problem is that many executives, agreeing with Drucker, know generally what their goal is, but they are in confusion as to how to attain it. There are many contributing factors to this confusion. One is that businessmen are being steeped in theory—Maslow, Herzberg, McGregor, etc. But there is too little empirical knowledge to show them what to do with the theory that they are told is so important. Recently I heard a psychologist tell a group of about four hundred OD personnel how essential it is to operate from a theory base in their change efforts. He left the distinct impression—I'm sure he didn't mean to—that it didn't really make much difference what theory base they choose.

Our preoccupation with theory—and the lack of knowledge of what to do with it—is undermining our effectiveness. More and more we can expect to find resistance among businessmen to the jargon and theory-spouting, especially when they come from well-meaning people who seem to believe that all that is necessary is to know the right words and concepts.

There are legitimate charges of faddism. Very often in companies I have noticed an air of "Let's try this for a year; then we'll try something else." Consequently the OD thrust is blunted by so much experimentation and variation —laboratories, sensitivity training, management by objectives—that no one can develop measurements to show the effectiveness of OD (a fact that resulted in widespread attrition among OD personnel when businesses cut down on expenses during the recent recession).

There is, of course, a need for experimentation, but there is also a need to understand and measure the success of what we are doing. The danger is that our organizations will find themselves expending energy, time, and money without knowing where they are. Or worse, they might suddenly find themselves almost out of business, as one company in Chicago did. The top management of the firm became so carried away by the new vistas in human relations that they neglected to run their business!

The confusion among businessmen, therefore, is understandable. But it isn't necessary. There is an excellent technique available for changing the culture of an organization. It can be safely experimented with. And the results from using it can be measured—almost immediately. What is surprising is that so few companies have used it to any significant extent.

The technique I refer to is the task force—interdisciplinary, interdepartmental—"organized," as Warren Bennis writes, "around problems to be solved by groups of relative strangers with diverse professional skills."[13]

Bennis refers to task forces as the temporary societies of the future. And indeed they will be, some time in the future, for managers who are content to be swept along by the fickle forces of change. For those managers who wish to control the direction of change in their organization, who want to see the effectiveness of their efforts in increased profits now, the task force provides a substantial bridge to the organization of the not-so-distant future.

It is already being used in a few corporations with considerable success. In the next chapter we'll see three task forces at work.

THREE

THE ANATOMY AND FUNCTION
OF A TASK FORCE

In 1967, The Research Institute of America, which publishes advisory and educational programs for businessmen, faced the perplexing failure of what was potentially its most profitable product. Management Membership, a program to help managers develop leadership skills, had been introduced in 1963. It was seen at that time as a highly effective, original approach to self-learning by those managers enrolled as members by their companies.

Considerable professional talent had contributed to its development. The price was competitive. From the beginning, Institute salesmen were enthusiastic about presenting it to executives.

Yet, four years after its introduction, Management Mem-

bership was in deep trouble. Sales volume had not been
sufficient even to amortize the costs of its creation.

The villain of the piece was *Report to Members,* a
weekly publication that was intended to form the backbone
of the membership program. Salesmen found it hard to
merchandise. Executives who were considering the program for their subordinate managers questioned whether
those managers would get any real help from the weekly
report.

Institute management realized that the complaints were
justified. The report lacked focus. The primary reason for
the failure of the report was organizational, one with which
any experienced executive can identify. There was a division
of responsibility: One editorial department was charged
with the administration of the membership program as a
whole, while another department had the specific responsibility for publishing the weekly report. A continuing controversy between the two departments not only affected
the content of the publication but prevented the building
of a permanent staff. A succession of managing editors
with no clear mandate, no staff to depend upon from week
to week, resorted to reprinting material that had already
appeared in other Institute publications designed for different purposes and audiences.

The problem was clear; so were the solutions, neither
without pain. On the one hand, management could junk the
unprofitable program, write off the loss, and start over;
this would be a costly answer, in terms of prestige as well
as money. The alternative was to keep the program going
while staff professionals worked to correct the faults of
the report. Unfortunately, there was a shortage of manpower to do the job.

Nevertheless, the decision was made to stay with the

membership and to try to remake the report into a distinctive publication. Six editors were asked to provide their talents on a part-time basis, to function as a task force to build a new report.

Five members of the task force represented both departments involved in the membership program and the production of the report. The sixth editor worked independently of both departments. Each had a different professional interest: one economist, one lawyer, one specialist in front-line supervisory training, one sales and marketing management expert, one analyst of government agency operations, and one specialist in industrial relations. In this particular task force, the specific disciplines were not as important as the fact that each member had his own perspective on the needs of the report's audience. (Interestingly, the final product designed by the task force did not noticeably represent any of the disciplines.) The task force elected to retain the name and the format of the existing report, rather than to create a new product. They limited their efforts to determining the content, the style, and the scope of the report.

The group set for itself a deadline six months from the date of the first meeting. It was agreed that a minimum of one meeting a week was realistic, and that other meetings could be called at the suggestion of any member. Work on the project outside the meetings was encouraged, as were discussions. But to prevent the forming of informal subgroups, members were asked to discuss outside developments in the formal sessions.

At the outset, the two division managers who supervised most of the editors in the group offered to sit in on task force meetings. They were asked by the group not to. But the managers *were* requested to serve as liaison with top management. Later, the group insisted on acting as their own liaison.

Barbara Whitmore, now one of the Institute's three division managers, describes the leadership problem faced by the task force. "In the first meetings, there were efforts on the part of some to appoint a permanent chairman and managing editor. In fact, I was favored, probably because I didn't belong to either department. But we successfully fought down those efforts. The solution we came up with was that each member of the group would serve as managing editor of the report for two weeks, during which time he would call and chair meetings. The point was that we needed every member of the group to contribute weekly to the publication. Obviously, no task force editor would overlook this obligation because he knew that, when he served as managing editor, he had to have the cooperation of his colleagues."

Although a great deal of professional talent and experience were brought to bear on a major problem in a limited time period, there was no interruption of the members' regularly assigned functions. One of the chief advantages of a task force is that those who participate in it need only contribute on a part-time basis. (The fact is that in most organizations highly talented people seldom are so burdened that they are unable to adjust their schedules to make even more output possible. Ironically, as many experienced managers know, the more a man has to offer, the proportionately less an organization tends to ask of him.)

After much debate, the majority rule approach, operative in so many committees, was discarded in favor of decisions that elicited the agreement of all members of the group. The rationale for consensus decisions was this: The objec-

tives could not be reached, it was felt, unless every participant agreed that what the group decided to do was in fact
the best way to get the job done. There would be no compromise, no going along.

In the weekly meetings each editor described the article
he hoped to contribute. The ensuing discussion usually
helped to shape and expand his idea. Later the finished
product would be commented on by each team member
before it was edited and printed by the current managing
editor. In their discussions and written criticism, the six
specialists, aware of their own differing interests, tried to
encourage contributions, the content of which would ap-
peal to all. Consequently, the focus of *Report to Members*
gradually became that of *behavior* on the job. The objective
of the report was now to help the manager achieve competence in his interactions with others.

The results were completely successful. The group reported its work done in less than the six months it had
scheduled for itself. It recommended that it be phased out,
at the same time presenting a plan for continuing the quality of the report that the group efforts had achieved. According to the task force plan, a separate editorial department was to be set up to take total charge of Management
Membership. Two of the editors on the task force were
designated as department head and managing editor, re-
spectively.

A further recommendation was that other members of
the group would continue to volunteer editorial contributions until the new department could be adequately staffed.
Eventually, *Report to Members* became one of the most
popular publications put out by the Research Institute. Not
only did it remain the heart of the Management Member-

ship program, but it was, under a different name, spun off
as a biweekly report sold by direct mail solicitation.

The Institute's task force is a prime example of how,
through collaboration that crosses departmental and disci-
plinary boundaries, any organization can temporarily concentrate its resources to get a problem solved without dis-
rupting its day-to-day activities. Says Barbara Whitmore,
"When I look back, it seems to me that we employed what
was for that time a radical technique. We didn't have a
model. But what we did have were a group of intelligent,
creative people, and a management enlightened enough to
give us the freedom to solve the problem in our own way.
The result was a very effective task force. We developed
our own model, which we've used since on other problems
and projects."

There are, however, some problems that are so complex,
that constitute such a threat to the well-being of an organization, that a full-time intensive approach to a solution has
to be designed—as in the case of a large, highly successful
manufacturing firm.

THE ADQ CORPORATION

In the early part of 1970, the top management of the
ADQ Corporation (the name is fictional) recognized the
potential disaster they faced. It was, of course, not an overnight development. There had been symptoms of growing
trouble for three years, but in a period of rapid expansion—
business volume had doubled since 1961—it was easy to
underestimate their seriousness or to procrastinate in devis-
ing solutions.

But the recession set ADQ's problems in bold letters. Customer dissatisfaction had reached epidemic proportions. Orders were filled improperly, were delivered late, or misshipped. Relationships with suppliers had become strained because of the frequent pressure put on them by ADQ to rush materials or to change the orders in process. Employee morale was low, due in part to negative feedback from customers, in part to the lack of planning and coordination by management.

The obvious culprit was the massive computerization undertaken by ADQ some years earlier. The company had realized that its computers were underutilized, although it had become the envy of other companies in the industry by computer regulation of purchasing functions, production schedules, inventory control, distribution, and shipping.

Unfortunately the computerization program never realized its potential. In the years of rapid growth, planning was inadequate and tended to be conservative in its projections. The training of data processing personnel was too narrowly focused: They were generally unaware of the nature and technology of the operations they were programming the computer to regulate. Managers in purchasing, production, marketing, etc., did not understand the importance of accuracy and completeness in supplying data needed for programming. People on the other end, struggling with outputs, were not able to feed back enough helpful information to correct the mistakes being made. And communications between line and staff were weak and faulty, due in large part to the feelings of superiority that staff personnel made little attempt to hide.

An emergency task force was assembled by the firm's top management from both line and staff functions: a manager from production and one from traffic, a data processing specialist, a systems analyst, and an engineer (who was also to function as leader). For the first three months of its existence, the task force met almost daily. The members concentrated their initial efforts in these three areas:

1. Defining the major problem areas—fourteen were eventually identified—and assigning responsibility for solutions to members of the group.

2. Building task force effectiveness. There were two levels of concern. Team members clearly saw the need to be educated in the technology relevant to the problem areas. Experts in these technologies met with the group in orientation sessions. Courses were arranged for the entire task force and for individuals. In addition to the information required to do the job, task force members studied their interactions, their ability to work together. A problem-solving, team-building laboratory was conducted, in which the group members participated in simulated management problems. After each problem or task, each participant rated his own effectiveness, that of each colleague, and that of the group as a whole, in dealing with that problem or task.

3. Creating a productive liaison with various divisions of the corporation whose cooperation is vital in furnishing the necessary inputs. As a preliminary step, a course in consulting skills—listening, and gathering, analyzing, and evaluating data—was held for the task force.

Each of the five members was given authority to build a staff to help him with his assigned responsibilities, the problem areas in which he was to concentrate. As an example, the engineer has three subgroups working under his direction, twenty-five people in all. The leader of each subgroup is part of a leader's group, headed by the engineer, who in turn is a member of the task force. It is a linking-pin structure.

The subgroups form and reform as necessary, as progress dictates a change in emphasis or assignments change. A member of an engineering subgroup may find himself on "temporary duty" in a systems or traffic subgroup.

As of this writing, the task force has functioned for eighteen months. Members meet every other week, and periodically they engage in two-day laboratory refresher sessions during which they again evaluate their effectiveness as a team. At the present time, the data already gathered and the success of the initial changes made indicate that it will be another eighteen months before the task force is satisfied that its data-gathering methods and criteria are realistic, that ongoing training programs are effectively established for all those responsible for supplying inputs and feedback, and that there is effective real-time data retrieval (the present batch processing is a temporary expedient). The task force will not be phased out and its members returned to their former responsibilities until the success of their efforts is clearly evident.

Each of the above temporary task forces was formed to find the solution to a problem which for a period of time was exclusively the temporary group's to work out. And in each case, in retrospect, the use of a task force seems logical, a slight variation of corporate structure and lines of authority.

By way of contrast, we take a look now at an unusual—and most people justifiably could say *radical*—use of a task force as a duplicate management structure.

THE HADDINGTON COMPANY

The Haddington Company (the name is fictional) is a West Coast subsidiary of a *Fortune* 500 corporation. In the summer of 1970, Haddington, a recent acquisition of the diversified parent company, was in deep trouble, losing a half million dollars each month.

A diagnosis made by the parent corporate management disclosed that the problem was *not* in the subsidiary's products or marketing. All evidence indicated that the fault lay almost entirely with Haddington's top management. They were not functioning effectively. Cooperation was virtually nonexistent. The diagnosis also disclosed that the president of the company had been rendered completely ineffective by the infighting of his managers. "There was nothing left to do but to cart off the corpse," observes Tom Stilwell (name changed), corporate director of organization development.

Performance appraisals of the remaining six resident managers showed that each was competent in his function. It was their relationships with each other that was killing the company, due in large part to the competition among the executives for the president's job.

One of the options available to Stilwell was, of course, that of replacing the troublesome managers with a new management team made up of capable men recruited from other parts of the huge corporation or even from outside. The rationale for replacement, of course, is that it would undoubtedly be easier to build a new team with strangers than to try to turn the present group around.

But Stilwell felt this somewhat traditional approach would be an unnecessary waste of human potential. Furthermore, the cure could be more quickly fatal than the disease. Not only did he want to keep the company running —he knew the resident managers had the ability to do that —but he wanted to start working on the managers' relationships immediately. And he couldn't have done either while breaking in a new team.

So Stilwell took a very bold step, one that could be disastrous if not handled correctly. He made up a task force of managers from various parts of the corporation, each duplicating the functions of the six managers left in the troubled company after the president was fired. Thus, for every responsibility in the management ranks, there were now *two* jobholders. Each resident manager had a backup man, a manager who knew the job but who, in rank, was slightly below the resident manager. There were two reasons for this disparity in rank: first, the temporary assignment would provide more of a challenge for him than for a more experienced manager of equal rank; and second, the task force member would be anxious to prove his ability to be promoted.

The outrage among the resident managers that followed this development is easy to understand. Stilwell fed the fire even more. He announced to all of the resident managers that not one of them, no matter how qualified, would be considered for the position of president. "After the anger died down," he reports, "there was a sigh of relief. At least now, nobody had to worry about one of the other managers in the company sneaking into the job."

From the moment the "reward" of their previous competitive efforts was removed, the infighting began to diminish. It did not, however, disappear for a time. Stilwell felt it was important to immediately institute an organization development program by which he could accomplish these goals:

* To help the resident managers understand why their relationships had been destructive;
* To guide them toward more collaboration, away from competition, with each other.
* To create a different climate for the company, one in which the managers could better achieve their objectives while promoting the good of the organization.

This was one of the reasons for the task force, to give the resident manager an opportunity to participate in laboratory and workshop sessions that were an integral part of the organization development. While the resident managers were engaged, their task force counterparts could mind the store. Actually, the relationship between the task force and resident managers was also calculated to be part of the learning and development experience for both sets of managers. In learning to collaborate with his task force counterpart, the resident manager, Stilwell hoped, would begin to learn how to build a more effective relationship with the other resident managers.

The *exact* authority of the task force members was not spelled out. They were "consultants" (and the residents were clients). But if the recommendations made by the "consultants" were ignored, they had the authority to press for the deficiencies to be corrected. It was the responsibility of both groups to work out some basis for collaboration.

The task force members were told that under no circumstances would any of them replace any resident manager who left or was fired. That reduced the possibility that competition would persuade a task force manager to make his counterpart look bad.

Of course, there was always the possibility that a resident manager couldn't pull it off, couldn't work in a collaborative atmosphere. He would have to be fired, and the task force manager would take over the responsibility until a permanent replacement could be found.

The fact that the task force was firmly in control and possessed the ultimate authority was evident in the fact that the task force leader, Tom Stilwell, took over the president's function until a permanent replacement could be found.

The first step in the organization development for the resident managers involved a "confrontation lab," designed by Stilwell, who had experience in running such sessions. Each manager was required to write a letter to each of the other five men he worked with, telling what that man did that he liked and thought effective, and what he didn't like and didn't feel effective.

The letters were exchanged with no verbal accompaniment, and each manager took the five letters and listed their pluses and minuses on a large chart. After he had recorded his "assets" and "liabilities" (as others saw them), all the managers were brought together. Each manager stood before his chart and talked about the good and bad things that his associates saw in him. Because they had had to write these things before talking about them, Stilwell says, the discussion was much more cool, less defensive than if they had verbalized from the beginning.

Other such sessions followed this initial confrontation in

which the resident managers continued to level with each other while busying themselves with the variety of problems facing their company and with the process of their work—*how* they were accomplishing what they were accomplishing.

At each session, a member of the corporate organization development staff, a professional with psychological training, was present to facilitate, to act as trainer when need be, or to act as leader when the group required it.

Building a duplicate management structure by using a task force is an unorthodox approach to the problem this company faced. The idea of two complete managerial structures performing one set of tasks may seem to be extravagant, but it was probably a great deal cheaper and less disruptive than firing the resident managers would have been.

Stilwell's unorthodox solution was a success because he had been quick to see that, if the resident managers could work out their interaction problems, there was no reason why they could not function effectively. And his prognosis was confirmed when, after only three months, he was able to recall the task force.

A new president was brought in, a man who was experienced in laboratory training and who could be relied upon to understand the process that was occurring. A year after the task force left, five of the original managers are functioning capably. One of the original six resigned after the task force left. The company is operating with a profit. And elsewhere in the corporation are six managers who shared operating responsibility for three months, who learned how to collaborate—and who learned the importance of collaboration.

THE IDEAL TASK FORCE

Groups, of course, are hardly new in the structure of business organizations. There have always been the staff and the committee. But for the most part staffs and committees are advisory bodies, subject to the authority of a higher manager who is free to accept or reject their work, and who has the real authority to act or not to act.

On the other hand, the task force is, as the name indicates, formed to *accomplish* a task. It is a temporary group, with temporary authority and responsibility. And the most distinctive feature of the task force is that its responsibility extends far beyond suggesting solutions or making recommendations. The true task force has *operational responsibility* for what it proposes. Its work is not done until there are instruments created (for example, a new department such as in the Research Institute case) to carry on its work. Nor should the task force be dissolved until it is certain that the work it has done has in fact provided a solution or feasible means. As we shall see, one of the principal reasons why task forces fail is that they are separated from the implementation of what they recommend, that they are not required to stand or fall with what they propose.

Another trademark of the task force is that it is *interdepartmental*. It cuts across departmental boundaries (and barriers). It is an instrument of collaboration. No important function in an organization can be done in a vacuum, without the assistance of others in other functions. As I have pointed out, a manager's responsibility is not matched by his authority—he needs the contributions of those over whom he has no authority. When problems of integrating efforts arise, the task force is an ideal instrument to resolve conflicts and to build collaboration.

Increasingly, task forces are *interdisciplinary*. The biochemist from research joins the sales manager, the marketer, the production manager, and the financial officer to determine what kind of product to bring to the marketplace considering the needs of the customer and the resources of the company; how that product can most efficiently be produced; and how many ways that product can serve a customer. The complexities of doing business today —the technology, the need for up-to-date accurate information, the coordination of many different skills and specialties—render it impossible that any one man or any group of men from any one function can ever know enough to confidently and successfully guide a corporation.

The task force enjoys a higher degree of *autonomy* than any other kind of group. Given its over-all objective—effective computerization, as in the ADQ case—the group should be as free as possible to establish its schedule, methods of collaboration, means of resolving the matter before it, and even in some situations to determine its own leadership. The task force members should be free from interference by their regular managers. The work of the group ideally should be placed under the umbrella of an executive powerful enough to provide protection for the group and to act as an authority reservoir.

Finally, within a task force decisions are made by *consensus*. Majority rule too often limits openness and commitment. The members of a task force should feel that whatever decision is made, whatever action taken, is probably the best that could be achieved given the circumstances, and is certainly superior to what any one member could achieve on his own.

Up to this point we have discussed the task force as an instrument of solving problems or creating new opportunities. But the "fallout" from the regular use of such groups can be enormously beneficial to the organization, as we shall see in the next chapter.

FOUR

SOME TASK FORCE BONUSES

A few years ago, top management at Riegel Textile Corporation, disillusioned with their training and development
programs, began to experiment with interdisciplinary, interdepartmental groups which, instead of working on classroom or simulated exercises, would tackle some of the real
problems Riegel faced. For example,

* What kind of management training is best for Riegel?
* Introducing minorities to the organization.
* Improving the work relations between two Riegel divi-
sions.
* Should Riegel own its warehouses?

From the outset, the enthusiasm of the managers on the first task force, the measurable learning that occurred, and the progress toward solving corporate problems, all convinced Riegel executives that they had discovered a potent new tool for upgrading their organization.

Each Riegel task force is appointed for two years. It is large; perhaps as many as twenty-five participants are selected. The group meets quarterly for two days. Thus the task force actually works together eight or nine times in its life, for an aggregate of two to three weeks. It operates under the guidance of Riegel's vice chairman of the board, with the help of the vice president of personnel and a consultant who was formerly a Riegel vice president.

Although these training groups explore real problems and seek real solutions, they do not have operating responsibility. They are thus one step away from being a task force in every sense of the word. They research, advise, and recommend. They have the authority to interview any Riegel executive or employee, to look into any aspect of the corporation's operation that relates to the task force's objective. However, once the group has presented its report to top management, its work is done.

The benefits, both to Riegel and to the task force members, are substantial and lasting. The firm recognized *immediate* profit from its training program: Most task force recommendations have been put to work successfully. There is a belief among Riegel's top management that the quality of the task force solutions and recommendations is probably higher than the decisions reached by a departmental or homogeneous group. As one executive puts it, "Task forces have a way of cutting through company dogma." An interdisciplinary, interdepartmental group usually is less respectful toward tradition and territory than departmental staffs and committees.

(This was the experience, incidentally, of a major international airline that had been experiencing severe crew scheduling problems. Flight personnel were overassigned on some flights, while other flights were undermanned, resulting in last-minute callups. There were cases in which crews reported for a nonexistent flight. Collaboration between flight and operations personnel and management was too weak for the problems to be confronted and solved. The breakthrough came when a task force was formed of representatives of all departments involved. In a matter of a few weeks, the part-time group had researched the problem and arrived at effective solutions accepted by all departments and by management.)

Another dividend from task forces that are consciously used for training is that the groups act as a management assessment center. The task force can provide many of the advantages of assessment centers without the disadvantages. Some of the purported advantages of centers in which employees' leadership skills and promotion potential can be measured are:

• The centers provide more objective data than an employee's managers, whose biases toward or against him could affect the validity of their evaluations.

• The uniformity of the simulated exercises and standards creates conditions of fairness and leads to more valid comparative data.

Aside from the fact that assessment centers are very expensive to design and maintain, there are these drawbacks:

• Assessors must be trained. Often these are line managers rather than professionals, and bias is still operative.

• Some candidates object to assessment centers because, in their opinion, like psychological testing, the centers invade privacy, create tension that may impede individual effectiveness, or are not as scientifically reliable as center proponents claim.

A MANAGEMENT RESERVOIR

The task force can create more realistic criteria for management selection than any other technique. In the first place, the testing is done in genuine risk situations. The stakes are real, as could be the rewards, and the behavior is significant. In a simulation, a man may be encouraged to take more chances than he would when facing risk, or his motivation to demonstrate his skills is lower because there is no expectancy of rapid feedback and reward for having done well. This argument, by the way, demonstrates to me the desirability of training through the means of *true* task forces—that is, giving them some degree of operating responsibility.

Second, the task force provides a variety of evaluation opportunities. In addition to an employee's regular manager, assessments can be obtained from the task force leader, from its other members, and, as in the case of Riegel, experienced executives who act as a resource to the group.

Looking beyond training, the organization that makes wide use of task forces goes a long way toward solving the problem of what to do with the man who cannot, at least for the time being, be promoted, or is unsuitable to be promoted further, or should actually be removed from his management position.

Most companies have the need to create a reservoir of potential managerial talent from which they can draw when openings occur. Some firms have two or three candidates for each management position, what is called 2X-ing and 3X-ing a job. The practice is wasteful, because some candidates get tired of the competition or of just waiting. They leave for opportunities elsewhere, as do those who lose out on the promotion when it is made.

The other extreme is not to prepare people at all to move up, which, of course, means developing managers after they have been promoted (and hoping they are developable). It is a practice widely followed, but there is little to recommend it. It is risky, inefficient, and expensive.

One solution is to keep the management potential busy on task forces. They may not yet have the title they seek, but they are progressing. They are enjoying authority far beyond what they would possess outside the group. They are learning and acquiring new skills. And, if their task forces function as they should, the managers-to-be have prestige and distinction within the organization. (It is quite logical to establish a hierarchy of task forces. The higher you go, the more important the problem, the greater the authority given the group, the more publicity given the membership.)

As I write, an article in *The New York Times* describes the unhappiness of managers who, because of politics or reorganization, are working at less than they are capable of doing. They "are frustrated by their inability to be promoted, disgruntled by their failure, critical of their bosses, and wary of their subordinates." They are casualties, and they are being buried before their time.

Of course, there are those who are justifiably on plateaus.

A large New York bank has organized into teams men who, for one reason or another, are not expected to rise higher in the organization. Each man has a regular assignment. But in the case of a sudden work overload or another kind of emergency in any department, a team of these employees is sent in to help the regular departmental personnel until the emergency has passed.

One of the most serious problems faced by nearly every business is the older manager who has retired on the job. He sits there on the shelf, blocking traffic, preventing those managers below him from moving up. Yet his knowledge and experience are still of value to the corporation. There is no reason just to let him sit there; and it is humiliating to give him a nonjob or a title of *consultant* or of *senior vice president*. If you are going to continue to pay him a salary, keep him contributing. Somewhere there is a task force to which he can contribute his knowledge and experience.

A corporation will find that task forces can aid its personnel staff in making sure its human resources are used fully. In the face of a challenge different from anything he has previously experienced, a man might call on skills that no one—himself included—knew he possessed. (Occasionally Riegel has reassigned employees who, during their task force experience, expressed interest in changing career directions—and demonstrated the ability to do so.)

MOTIVATION THROUGH LEARNING

Nearly everyone needs challenge, a chance to accomplish, to grow and stretch himself. It has always surprised me that so few executives seem to realize the motivational power of a learning situation. Herzberg presents an interesting argument that people who are expanding their knowledge of and skill in doing their jobs are motivated. They don't have to be manipulated, kicked, persuaded. They have all the inner force they need to move.

Actually, psychologists have been telling us for years that the most effective learning is when there is a problem or a goal. What a man does depends in large part on his expectancy that his behavior will result in solving a problem or achieving a goal (which could include a reward).

The problem with classroom learning is that the student is often unable to see the reward of his behaving in a certain way. Why should he? Where is the problem or the goal? On the job, however, he experiments with his behavior so as to achieve certain results. For example, he perceives there is a good chance that, if he acts toward a colleague in a warm, friendly manner, the other man will be receptive to working with him. He tests his assumption by behaving in a warm, friendly manner. He receives "feedback" from his colleague. If the other man responds positively, agrees to work together, then our man is encouraged to behave in a warm, friendly manner in the next situation that is similar. So, for effective learning, we have a perception, an expectancy, feedback, and reinforcement. The closer in time the feedback and reinforcement are to the behavior, the greater is the chance that learning will take place.

A task force, with its goal and the expectancy of its members, with almost simultaneous feedback and reinforcement of effective behavior, sets up a much superior learning situation than most classrooms can provide. Most classroom-type education prepares for contingencies that may never occur. It is, as we have already pointed out, based on the standards or activities of others in the past. The pragmatic, on-the-job education of the task force involves here-

and-now risk, and is individualized, fitted to the needs and abilities of the man doing the learning.

It's hard to shake the notion, rooted in tradition, that the proper place to learn how to manage is on the university campus or in centers such as the American Management Association sponsors. Management skills, because they involve interaction with people within a certain context, cannot be taught *in vacuo*. The essence of good management—interpersonal competence—can be effectively learned only in the manager's working environment. It is there he finds his goals, and within that context he experiments with behavior he thinks will help him achieve his objective. He gets the feedback and reinforcement from those with whom he must interact.

JOB ENRICHMENT

What Frederick Herzberg will probably be remembered longest for is the concept of *job enrichment*. The concept derives from the motivators or satisfiers: the work itself, achievement, advancement. The point of job enrichment is to provide a challenge to the employee, to make his work important and interesting, to keep him in a learning situation, to enable him to exercise some control over the content of the job.

So far in the history of job enrichment we have not heard about enriching managerial jobs. One consultant said to me, rather cynically, "What company wants to admit that its managers need job enrichment?" I put the question to the training director of a New York bank. His answer: "We do." It is rare candor. This corporation began its job enrichment at the lowest level, where most such programs begin. In trying to give more responsibility to clerical workers, such as typists and keypunch operators, management found they had to "borrow" from the duties performed by their supervisors, duties that those supervisors had formerly performed at lower levels and that they had taken with them as they rose in the hierarchy. Once the supervisors were stripped of work they should not have been permitted to do, they were faced with the necessity to manage the essential—but neglected—content of their jobs.

The New York bank's experience provides a good argument for job enrichment at all levels of an organization. But, of course, purging a manager's job of the responsibilities he should no longer have is a minor part of the argument. The most important reasons to enrich a man's job are to get more for your money, if you are the boss, and for him to have the opportunity to show what he can do. After all, if Maslow is right, we are not really fulfilled until we become what we are capable of being. So the wise thing for a manager is to keep piling it on, to present as many challenges and as much variety as the man can take.

Unfortunately, too often, what a manager gives a subordinate is what the manager is willing to give up—it has little to do with what the subordinate is capable of handling. Probably the most common complaint uttered by the ambitious manager is that his boss won't let go of authority, won't delegate.

The part-time task force is a good way of "loading," of putting more significant content into a man's job. Ironically, it may be too effective as a job enrichment tool—by contrast, the task force member may find his regular job unexciting, a problem we'll discuss in the next chapter.

But the general phenomenon of boredom is an issue that few executives seem to confront. A refreshing exception is the Texas multimillionaire, H. Ross Perot, who has been quoted by *The New York Times* as saying, "When you consider the impact that his work has on him and his family, the company has a moral obligation to be an exciting place for an employee."

Who would dare to disagree with that? Yet, look at the conditions that prevail. We stick a man in a job, define for him the limits of his authority and responsibility, and leave him there for several years. By the end of say two years, he has mastered probably 80 percent of his job, and he is condemned to spend several more years learning how to do the other 20 percent. He becomes bored and suffers from obsolescence (because, since he cannot expand, his energy must be invested in continuing to do what he has always done). Eventually, a position of greater responsibility in the hierarchy is available and we promote the man. Now the process starts all over again, except that his waiting time in all likelihood will be extended: The higher one goes in the pyramid, the fewer the opportunities for advancement.

No small wonder, then, that we see a trend today: Managers are leaving their comfortable, well-paying, prestigious jobs to look for second careers—to teach, to enter public service, to set themselves up in businesses of their own, anything to escape the exponential increase of boredom.

(One of my favorite people, a salesman in his sixties, year after year figured among the leading producers in his company. He had returned to sales after a successful business career heading his own firm. His financial resources were considerable, his needs modest. I asked him why he kept working as hard as he did. His response: "Because this way I keep learning; and when I stop learning, I'll die.")

FORMALIZING THE INFORMAL

Of course, leaving a job is only one way to escape, another being to "leave" the job while staying on the payroll.
The thrust of a man's creativity is not blunted by the organization; it is simply diverted. We are all familiar with
the man who puts in his time at the office, then goes to his
real love: to sit on the town council, to meet with the Boy
Scouts council, to serve on a community committee, or
to work on a small business he has started.

What we are less familiar with is the informal group that
exists within the formal structure. Likert is right to say that
the authoritarian model is an especially fertile breeding
ground for such groups, bound by a common objective
that often runs counter to the formal organization's goals.
People want the security of belonging to a compatible group,
in which they can offset the relative lack of concern and
the impersonality of the over-all organization.

What little has been written about informal groups—
and it is little—has been concerned largely with the rank-
and-file. But people at every level band together in such
groups, and the counterproductive effort (in terms of total
organizational effectiveness) can be far more damaging in
the higher echelons. The president of an international airline recently informed his four senior vice presidents that
he would choose his successor from among them. The corporation, whose losses for the past two years are alarming,
is now torn by dissension. The four vice presidents, as
might be imagined, are actively competing with each other.
But throughout the entire organization, partisan groups
have formed to advance the cause of their favored "can-

didate," and with rare exceptions, their activities are obstructive and divisive.

It's admittedly an extreme case of what can happen. Usually informal groups are not ad hoc, and exist quietly. Nevertheless, the manager who either ignores them or acts contrary to their "welfare" does so at his peril. Management is better advised to work in concert with this quite human desire to band together, to belong, to achieve a group identity. And through task forces, management can assure itself that the group's goals advance those of the organization rather than inhibit them.

BLURRING THE LINES

There are three additional benefits accruing from the use of task forces that we should mention:

1. Perhaps the most common frustration experienced by a manager (unless he is sitting at the very top of the pyramid) is that, in the bureaucracy, his authority seldom matches his responsibility. A flagrant example: A magazine publisher requires the managing editors of its three publications to share editorial personnel. Thus, each managing editor must arrange for the time and talents of the same people his two colleagues must call upon also. He cannot, on his own, *require* anyone belonging to the editorial pool to contribute. Nor can he hire, fire, discipline, or reward. Yet, his responsibility is to publish a magazine. But he has no authority over the people whose cooperation he must have.

The task force enjoys a unique advantage in that its authority is equal to its responsibility. Furthermore, that authority is granted temporarily, long enough for the group to do the job. Of course, it is disturbing for traditionalists to envision the shifting of power centers. There is something "untidy" about it. But the problems and opportunities don't always come from one direction, and through task forces the organization can apply optimum strength and resources to meet and take care of whatever challenges it. It's a far more practical approach than trying to change the formal organization, reassign titles and staffs, and write new position descriptions each time the unusual occurs. It is certainly far superior to the necessity of having the chairman, president, or executive vice president in on every project to insure sufficient authority to do the job.

2. There's no question that the interdepartmental, interdisciplinary task force can substantially improve horizontal communications within an organization. What is often overlooked is that a task force improves communications upward as well. It pushes ideas up the line with more authority and weight than an individual manager or department can usually muster. This was the discovery of some American Airlines supervisors at a station where American planned some physical changes. The supervisors, representing such functions as ramp and passenger service, had their own ideas as to what, at the station, would constitute a more efficient setup. Representative supervisors, with the permission of higher management, formed a task force, studied their own needs and American's plans for modification, and then devised their own recommendations, most of which American accepted.

I'm not suggesting that the airline would not have entertained suggestions from an individual manager. But it's undeniable that the task force communications had two clear advantages: first, the recommendations reflected the wishes and needs of many, and second, the recommendations had been tested against the wishes and needs of *each* department. What emerged bore the stamp of conviction that the suggestions were feasible for the entire station.

3. The distribution of authority and the effectiveness of communications—both have profound influences on an organization's ability not only to survive but to prosper— and so does the relationship between line and staff (usually hampered by authority and communications deficiencies). Once again, this is a military legacy that has probably done more damage than good in our business organizations. The new trend, incidentally, of recruiting Organization Development personnel from line management is, at once, an admission that staff people have neither the knowledge nor "clout" necessary to influence line personnel, and a healthy blurring of the distinction between the two traditional divisions (and antagonists).

Staff managers often manifest a sense of superiority to line managers. The former like to think of themselves as the intellectual force, with expertness in a specialty their credentials. Line managers counter with a superiority of their own: They can clearly render the staff "interlopers" ineffective if what staff proposes is not in accord with the line managers' "more experienced" perception of their needs.

So it goes. The fact is that both temperaments are needed in a business enterprise: the scholars and the pragmatists, the specialists and the generalists, the overviewers and the narrow viewers. In most organizations, the best relationship that has been achieved thus far is from maintaining consultant and client roles. It's a poor solution. Staff and line managers should be placed on the same task forces to operate with the same authority and responsibility, to agree on the same goals and means to achieve those goals. They have much to teach each other, much to learn from each other.

Perhaps if we can make it easier for staff and line managers to collaborate as equals, we can eventually do away with the artificial, wasteful barriers between them.

Thus the task force provides benefits beyond solving problems and making decisions that exceed the resources that any one function, department, or discipline can muster. Its value in assessing, training, and developing management, in expanding talents that exist in potential, in enriching jobs at all levels, improving communications, and building collaboration, is inestimable.

Even more important, we are facing a profound cultural change in moving from a pyramidal-bureaucratic-authoritarian model to the democratic-decentralized-temporary group society, a change in which the task force can play a vital role. And the evolution presents us with some very serious problems, some more real than others, however. In the next chapter we look at these problems as well as the suspicions expressed by experienced managers that the task force as a cure could be more painful than the disease.

FIVE

QUESTIONS AND OBJECTIONS

There have been many serious questions—and objections—raised as to the true effectiveness of the task force, both as a technique for utilizing resources now not being used properly and as a means for effecting organizational change. Some of the objections are rooted in misunderstanding and inexperience (or *bad* experience). Others show an understandable concern that many executives have in realizing that an extensive resort to task forces could have disruptive consequences for rigid organizations. As an example of this last point, consider the first question below:

1. If an organization is made up of many task forces, won't the results be anarchy? No one will know where the

authority is, where his responsibility stops and someone else's begins.

The evolution we speak of is not toward a completely free-form organization. There will probably always be a hierarchical structure, however simplified. The task forces obviously have to get their authority from *someone*. And an executive will have to act as liaison, coordinator—even traffic policeman—to insure that the task force's work is in the proper perspective, contributes to the whole rather than disrupts, is unique rather than a duplication, that the group's relationships with other groups and departments are collaborative rather than conflicting.

There are other reasons why there must be a command matrix that supports task force activity. First, there will always be certain functions that are easily routinized and programmed, functions that will not benefit from task forces. Second, task forces are by definition temporary groups. At least while corporations are developing the know-how and experience in using them, there will have to be functions that provide a substantial anatomy.

There is no question that from time to time the assignment given a task force will invade a manager's turf. If the group's objective is chiefly to make up the manager's deficiencies, it seems useless to worry about the conflict. The more commonly observed situation is one in which the task force tackles a problem that the manager has not had the authority or the resources to solve. Usually higher management will ask him to join the group so he can have a say in generating the solution to his problem.

There will be times when a manager cannot be spared from his regular functions—for example, when the task force is a full-time one. He should, however, be represented in the group by a man he chooses, one who can be expected to look out for his interest and keep him informed. Still, a great deal of diplomacy may be required —he is about to lose a chunk of his operation. The sweetener may be that, after a period of time, he will get it back without the problems that may have plagued him for so long. Or he may find that, thanks to the task force, his "new" operation will be much enlarged, or more important, with considerably more authority.

The best answer for the manager whose jurisdiction is about to be cut is a cultural one: If he understands the value of task forces, perhaps from having served on one, and if he knows that increasingly that is where the action is (for him, too), then his resistance will be lowered.

2. Task forces will create heavy expenses because the corporation will, in effect, have to maintain two structures.

Most corporations today have at least two structures: formal and informal, line and staff, etc. In fact, dichotomies and partitions exist in plenitude. Many of them are traditional, artificial, or political. And often they serve to inhibit an effective flow of information and to obstruct collaboration. The organization that strives to achieve more flexibility and fluidity through task forces will find itself reducing these partitions to a manageable minimum.

The corporation will have to weigh the successes and failures of the present system against the benefits and the liabilities of the looser structure with its temporary groups.

3. Aren't there a lot of headaches when a man works for two bosses: the task force leader and his regular manager?

Undoubtedly. Most of the problem involves where the employee invests his time and energy. And there is the danger that he will let his part-time commitment to the task force become full-time, to the chagrin of his regular boss and to the detriment of his assigned duties. (On a full-time task force there would be no such problem; he would be detached temporarily from his regular job.)

At the risk of being accused of glibness, let me say that in most situations this problem will exist more in anticipation than in actuality. The image of the overworked manager with not another minute to spare is largely a myth. And many managers who try to perpetuate that image do so because they are incompetent in their jobs or underutilized, and they don't want the fact recognized. Most organizations seldom strain their manager's capacities.

The task force's timetable should be developed from a realistic appraisal of what will be demanded of its members. If the load becomes greater than anyone had foreseen, then the schedule should be lengthened or the group should consider becoming a full-time one.

There will probably be individual conflicts, usually involving poor judgment, as, for example, the case of the manager who gets carried away by the excitement of the task force to the point where he neglects his permanent job. Such a conflict calls for confronting the issue. The task force leader should take some initiative, if only because he could at one time or another be in a position similar to that of the regular manager. Between the task force leader, the member, and the regular manager, an agreement must be reached as to what the man is expected to do in his permanent assignment in order to stay on the task force.

This kind of problem, incidentally, is one reason why—and we shall discuss this later in the chapter—a task force member's manager must be responsible for evaluation and salary review.

4. Won't full-time task force members worry about what

is going on in their regular departments while they're gone? Perhaps they won't have jobs to go back to, or much of their jobs will have been delegated to others.

Some anxiety will exist because the task force member will wonder whether his department can get along without him, but just as much, if not more, will be generated by his fear that they will get along very well—too well. If the latter is true, it is usually indicative of two harsh facts: First, there is a low level of trust between the absent task force member and his permanent boss; and second, the regular manager hasn't been doing what he should have been doing all along—arranging for fill-ins and replacements for his key employees.

If a manager stressed as a rule the necessity to have other people available to do a key man's work when that man was ill, or on vacation, or on leave of absence—or had quit, then one of his employees assigned to temporary duty outside the department wouldn't have extreme anxiety about his sudden dispensability.

It may well be that the man on a *full-time* task force should be thinking about *not* going back to his old assignment, that his future would be more productively spent elsewhere. One advantage of a team organization is that it exposes a man to different kinds of careers and provides opportunities to switch career directions. At any rate, the task force work that the man is doing now should be for the moment the most important to him. If it is not, then he is out of place, perhaps for other task forces as well.

5. Task force members may find their regular jobs unexciting by comparison with their temporary experience.

True, and every manager should recognize the phenomenon: After a successful, exhilarating team collaboration, there is a psychological letdown. It's quite normal, even after a part-time assignment. Depending on the man, his manager might be able to help him by recommending a little time off, or a work schedule that is light enough to permit him to make the transition, or in some cases an immediate, challenging job to help him out of his slump. The manager has to know his man to prescribe the remedy.

However, if the feeling persists, then the man ought to be given a chance to restructure his job, take on a new or enlarged responsibility, or consider different work. After all, his dissatisfaction isn't really new or generated by the task force. It was very likely there all the time—but well disguised.

6. Some people don't work well in groups.

Most people don't work well in groups, because they haven't been trained to do so. And some perform better by themselves, or in a one-to-one relationship than they do as part of a group. Temperamentally they are loners, or they may not have the emotional security to maintain the close emotional relationship that is part of a successful group collaboration. Whatever the reason, they usually don't make good managers, either.

The place for him is in a job that does not call for heavy interaction with others: research, accounting, etc. There is no reason, in the organization of the future, why this kind of employee would not be considered an important resource. But he will not be in the mainstream, and he will probably not be managerial potential.

7. Won't task force members develop an elitist self-image?

That's an understandable result in a company where task forces are where the action is, where successful task force experience is the key to advancement within the organization. When temporary team assignments become more common, the less will employees be inclined to demonstrate elitism. Nevertheless, there doesn't seem to be anything seriously wrong when a man is anxious to prove himself capable of joining a task force dealing with more complex, more prestigious issues than he has heretofore had a chance to work on.

In short, there will undoubtedly be certain task forces that will earn a man more valuable "service ribbons" than other groups, and he should be encouraged to try to move up to such assignments.

8. Task force members will be disruptive in their regular departments with their candor and openness.

Anyone who has ever seen a colleague freshly returned from sensitivity training or an encounter group knows what it is to endure a man who has just found religion. He has just come from a climate that encouraged—indeed, demanded—that people be open and candid in expressing their feelings, about themselves and about each other. He is still in his euphoria when he returns to an atmosphere that does not promote openness and candor, and it is usually a frustrating experience for him.

Trust, the basis for openness, is essential to any collaboration, such as a task force is. But the degree of trust in a collaborative group will usually far outstrip that found in most departments of an organization. Having experienced the pleasure in being open with others, having seen how constructive candor can be in human interaction, the task force member will try to practice his newly found virtues in his home environment.

The consequences of his cultural transplant will be less disruptive as increasing numbers of people build the trust that permits the expression of feelings, because of the emphasis on group consensus and team-building throughout the organization and the widening of task force experience.

9. Consensus is a slow way to get a decision.

Getting consensus can be slower than resorting to majority vote or unilateral decisions. But the slowness that is characteristic of consensus produces valuable benefits. First, everyone's views are aired, interests surface. No one feels left out. Second, the decision is one that everyone identifies with. It's not a compromise, where everyone has to give up something (usually what he most wants). Rather, a consensus decision is one that everyone who has participated in making it feels is the best decision that could have been made. Third, there is much evidence that group decisions made by consensus are usually of higher quality than the best decision offered by any one member of the group.

An example of this last point is the so-called NASA exercise, a simulation that many groups of businessmen have experienced. The group members are told that they are part of a moon expedition and that their craft has crash-landed two hundred miles from their base. They are given a list of equipment in the craft and are asked individually to rank each piece in order of importance to their survival on the journey to the base. Then as a group they come up with a ranking.

After a group has engaged in the exercise, the individual rankings are recorded, the group ranking is written down, and both are compared with the official NASA ranking. It's common to find that the consensus decision is closer to the official ranking than the best individual ranking.

The last important benefit of a consensus decision is that the people who have made it are committed to it. They can't withdraw—it represents their best efforts. They don't "just go along." It's too important for them in implementation to *prove* that their decision is a good one.

10. Task forces get so wrapped up in "process" that they don't get things done.

This is a subject that we'll come back to when we discuss laboratory training and its value in building effective teams (see Chapter Six). The term "process" denotes how an action is carried on. It does not refer to the content of the decision, rather the way in which the decision-makers interact. In a group members are urged not only to do something but to observe *how* they do it, to assess the behavior they see. By studying how they work together, a group can become more effective by repeating the behavior that is most effective.

It may happen that a group will get hung up so much on *how* they are working that they don't get the real work done, which is probably an avoidance technique. What is far more likely, however, is that a group will not work as effectively as it can because the members do not get sufficiently involved in the process.

11. In an organization where task forces are commonplace, the regular manager is the man who carries the burden, since he is vulnerable to raids on his talent.

True, but he will then be forced to do what he should have done before: develop pinch-hitters and replacement talent.

Actually one of the major manpower problems faced by a bureaucratic organization is that of buried or unknown talent. A valuable, promising employee finds himself locked in a particular department because only his manager knows how good that employee really is and is reluctant to let him go on to better things elsewhere.

In a team-oriented organization, the emphasis is on developing and furthering the resources it already possesses, even though such emphasis will at times result in inconvenience to managers who have to surrender employees. When managers are judged on the numbers of "comers" they produce for the rest of the organization, then managers will stop thinking so much about inconvenience and more about how to encourage the advancement of those who report to them.

Even so, the feeling of a manager that he has been *raided* can be lessened by negotiation. Sweden's state-controlled LKAB, a mining company, requires that its task force managers negotiate directly with divisional and functional heads for the specialists they need on their teams. Negotiation is preferable to the commandeering of talent by higher authority.

12. Is individual creativity lessened or even squelched in a group?

There is a phenomenon frequently observable in a group seeking a solution to a problem: They will tend to settle on one particular answer early in their discussion, even before all possibilities have been explored. Unless the members of the group value consensus, they won't insist on developing alternatives, on confronting all possibilities, however remote. Thus, members of a group will often do much better in developing ideas and possible solutions *individually* than they will in a group. That same group, however, is usually superior to the individual in evaluating ideas already proposed. (However, a group's effectiveness in the ideational phase can be developed.)

A group can make a unique contribution to individual creativity through the immediate feedback and recognition. One person's ideas are evaluated by the group, his assumptions are tested in the interaction of members, and he receives feedback on how his fellow task force members feel about what he has proposed—immediate reinforcement that can encourage a repetition of his creative behavior.

Thus, the group offers a faster and a surer reward for creativity than is generally found outside it. Perhaps the most significant encouragement given the innovator is his knowledge that the group has the authority to implement his idea if it is accepted.

The authoritarian model is full of nooks and crannies into which the innovator's contribution can disappear. Evaluation of his idea often takes place a considerable time after he proposed it and at a distance from him. And he may never receive any feedback on it.

13. Wouldn't an individual become less responsible and more reckless, because he is under the mantle of a group?

The immediate feedback we talked about in the previous question serves to blunt any tendency to cast off individual responsibility. A member's actions have an influence on the welfare and the effectiveness of the group. If anything, a man will feel an increased sense of responsibility because others are involved with him. Furthermore, in an effectively functioning task force, the controls that exist on the behavior of any member are those to which he himself has given assent.

14. Can't a task force easily become a runaway, exceeding its authority?

Not if there is a clear agreement on its goals, on the extent of its authority, if there is responsible leadership both in and outside the group. And, of course, in a System 4 organization (see Chapter Two), as Likert describes it, the one group will be linked with other groups and will be able to achieve its goals only in collaboration with other groups.

The more frequent problem is that a task force will not receive as much authority as it needs to properly do the job. The experiences of several task forces spring to mind: The goals were clear, the members were competent, the work was applauded throughout the organization. Unfortunately, the task force was not given operational authority, and top management found ways not to take action. One persistent and aggressive task force leader insisted on a meeting between his group and members of top management so that the executives could explain to the task force why their recommendations were not put into effect.

15. People need territory and status symbols, and in a team-oriented organization, they would have to give them up.

People tend to place greater emphasis on the nonproductive aspects of the job when, for internal and/or external reasons, they cannot be as productive as they wish or as the job demands. A man should be encouraged to carve out his niche, to make a unique contribution. But the real trouble begins when the organization conspires with the man to protect his territory.

True status comes from competence and achievement. If organizations begin to hew to that line, look out: People will be clamoring, pushing and shoving to get things done!

16. Temporary task forces will be expensive and inconvenient, since people will have to be sent here and there at company expense and be away from their home bases for long periods of time.

A European corporation that is part of an international conglomerate installed a computer and began to run into all sorts of expensive problems. The conglomerate contributed a task force of five high-level men—a task force leader plus a specialist in the following fields: production control, inventory control, data systems, and industrial engineering. Five months were required for his full-time task force to solve the problems of the European company. Of course, it was expensive and inconvenient—to the conglomerate, to the men, and to their families.

The question is whether the temporary task force is a more economical way to solve problems than to replace erring management or to retain consultants (who have no vested interest). And there's another consideration: In order to expose up-and-coming managers to a variety of training situations, environments, responsibilities, etc., many companies have insisted that their managers accept transfers around the United States and around the world. Not only is this expensive, but managers are beginning to resist the uprooting.

The task force may prove to be far less expensive and inconvenient than the present alternatives.

17. Management-by-objectives is more difficult to achieve when task forces are extensively used.

Actually, a management-by-objectives (MBO) system will be reinforced by task forces. First, members of teams will be establishing objectives on two levels: with their permanent managers and through the groups to which they belong.

Second, membership in task forces will give employees greater opportunity to benefit from MBO than they usually enjoy in more bureaucratic structures. To explain, we should recognize that many MBO programs are crippled because management sees them chiefly as a vehicle for translating organizational goals downward. But there is another direction MBO should take: helping the employee to define his personal goals and showing him, in the organizational context, how he can achieve them. And it is very often in a collaborative, democratic group situation that the definition and achievement of his individual objectives are more feasible.

Third, problem-solving and innovation are far more important in MBO than simply extending or refining what is already being done. And, of course, a task force is totally committed to solving problems and finding new opportunities.

Thus MBO is not only compatible in a team-oriented organization, it is also reinforced by it.

18. Team structure plays havoc with wage and salary policies. Who determines who gets paid how much for doing what?

If wage and salary policy is to create uniformity at all levels with standard differentials between levels, then it's doubtful that any wage-and-salary administrator will be very happy in a task force structure.

However, if the organization believes in recognizing and rewarding good performance with money, then management can be very comfortable with task forces. Not only do they provide opportunities for performance that is superior to what is expected or possible in most bureaucratic structures, but task forces also provide increased inputs for the man who has to pass on salary increases.

If the people he has lent to task forces do extraordinarily well, then the permanent manager may find himself under pressure to provide substantially higher salaries, which could be a strain on the budget, especially since he doesn't have full-time use of his "loans." But in time that kind of strain on the budget, and his vulnerability to being asked for more people to serve on task forces, may provide solid indication that he is a superlative manager.

Who should determine compensation? In some companies that regularly use task forces, he is the employee's permanent or regular manager. He has the budget. He receives performance evaluations from the task force leader —and from the other members, in some cases. He combines these data with his own judgment of the employee's effectiveness and arrives at a figure.

Where the task force is full-time and operative for an extended period (say, for more than six months), the senior manager responsible for the task force may be vested with merit increase decisions. This is especially recommended when the assignment of task force members after the group has finished is in question; that is, some may go on to duties different from those they had before participating in the task force (some members may be assigned to continuing the work of the task force on a permanent basis).

But in the majority of cases we can assume that the regular manager retains the responsibility for salary decisions, although he is expected to use the evaluations from the task force in those decisions.

19. Individual performance is harder to evaluate when an employee shuttles between his regular duties and a task force.

It should be *easier* to appraise. Certainly it should be easier to achieve more objectivity. In a later chapter we shall discuss the kinds of questions a company can ask in an appraisal system in which several appraisers contribute.

Of course, performance is only one aspect of appraisal. Higher management, through an appraisal program, is taking inventory of its personnel resources—their training and experience, their objectives (professional *and* personal), and their promotion potential. When you are able to observe an employee in a variety of work and interaction situations, you take out a lot of the guesswork that char-

acterizes employee evaluation in so many organizations today.

20. Task forces corrupt. They come up with ideas, but
those who have to implement the ideas are the ones who
bear the burden if those ideas are not feasible.

The argument of *corruption* has to do with the attitudes
that may develop in a man who feels free to develop solutions without being charged with the responsibility to see
that they work—a complaint frequently leveled against
consultants.

This objection is justified, because many companies with-
hold from their task forces operational responsibility for
the recommendations they have come up with. Members of
a task force should be accountable for their work. This accountability can be achieved in several ways:

a. *As overseers.* Although the day-to-day responsibilities
for carrying out the task force recommendations fall on
others, the group continues to monitor the operation. Their
role may be similar to that of a board of directors, or higher
management, or a resource, such as internal consultants
play. Each of these roles involves a differing degree of involvement in the actual implementation, but whatever the
extent of the involvement, the task force should be kept in
existence until its work has been demonstrated to be effective.

Recently, Yarway Corporation, a manufacturer in Blue
Bell, Pennsylvania, faced the problem of disappointingly
small profits on one of their product lines. Under the aegis
of the operating vice presidents, who meet every Friday
morning, a task force was formed of representatives from
marketing, cost accounting, product development, and
manufacturing engineering.

The task force was asked to define the problem and its causes and to develop solutions. What steps the task force felt should be taken were presented to a general meeting: task force members, the vice presidents, and other managers who would be involved in implementing the group's recommendations were present.

The recommendations were discussed at this general meeting: How many were to be accepted and implemented? The important thing is that the task force was there to discuss, clarify, and argue for its work. It did not simply make recommendations that can get sidetracked, disappear in the mist, etc. It was in on the decision-making process.

Once the decision was made, responsibility was fixed by the vice presidents. Who is responsible for what within what time period?

The task force remained in existence, meeting as often as was necessary, giving reports to the v.p.s at three-month intervals. The task force monitored and if necessary coordinated progress, acted as an information center, measured results, and dealt with problems that arose during implementation.

Two things are especially noteworthy: First, the task force operated under high-level authority, and second, the task force was not phased out until its recommendations had been demonstrated to be effective. The task force, to this extent, carried operational responsibility.

b. *As the operating group*. Here the roles that a task force plays vary widely. The Research Institute's editorial task force, described in Chapter Three, is an example of temporary but complete operational responsibility within the existing corporate structure.

The aerospace industry has become known for another kind of operational responsibility: the project team. A project manager may have extensive authority—for budget, personnel selection, and for dealing with the customer and subcontractors. Because the aerospace industry has largely been concerned with projects that come and go, begin and end, companies in that business have a more fluid structure than other corporations, a matrix consisting largely of such project groups. Some of these project groups are so independent and self-contained that when the project is terminated, many of its members are out of work.

Companies outside the aerospace industry have experimented with *venture* task forces. When a promising new business area is recognized, a task force is organized to study the ideas and to recommend a "go" or "no go." If the company decides to enter the new area, the task force becomes the nucleus of management and operates as a subsidiary company.

If the task force venture proves successful, a permanent operating company is formed. If unsuccessful, the task force is dissolved, and its members return to their regular responsibilities. There has been a minimum of disruption in the parent organization.

Not long ago, the International Basic Economy Corporation (IBEC), which had a mutual funds sales subsidiary in Spain, set out to explore the feasibility of a worldwide financial services organization. A venture group was formed: the chairman of IBEC, the area vice president in Spain, the director of the financial analysis department in New York, and the twenty-seven-year-old sales manager from the Spanish company, plus legal, accounting, and tax specialists as needed. The area vice president was chairman. The team recommended expansion, and set up an operation in Italy similar to that in Spain. The young sales manager was selected to head the new company as managing director.

Presumably any further international expansion will follow this pattern: venture task forces selecting the new area of operation, setting up a structure, and supplying a management nucleus.

Thus there are many levels of accountability, many degrees of involvement, in implementation of task force recommendations. The task force that is not held responsible for its actions does not have to stand or fall with its ideas and represents an inefficient use of an organization's personnel resources.

In this chapter I have reviewed some of the questions executives may raise about the extensive use of task forces. I haven't tried to disguise the fact that I do not regard some of those questions as really justified. Nevertheless, I am fully cognizant that what questions such as these reveal is a profound concern with the *cultural* changes that a team-oriented organization faces. The profitable use of task forces is not achieved simply by calling together a group of people and giving them their head. Nor is it accomplished by the well-meaning feeling in executives that "we must be more decentralized and democratic."

There must, of course, be the intention to restructure the organization. But people who are to function effectively in group problem-solving and decision-making must be trained to do so. Consequently, in the next chapters, our attention will be directed to that behavior in task force members that must be developed—or discouraged—so that a task force can achieve its objectives.

SIX

GROUP EFFECTIVENESS
THROUGH LABORATORY TRAINING

One approach to helping people be more effective in groups is that of the T (for training) group or the laboratory. Many people, when T group or lab is mentioned, think of sensitivity training. There has been a great deal of nonsense written about sensitivity training. But there is a great deal of nonsense *in* sensitivity training.

To begin with, most sensitivity training is not training at all. It is more properly described as an experience, one that may produce some learning as to one's behavior. But sensitivity training, as such, has little value in training people to be more effective in dealing with others in an organization. There are, however, certain kinds of laboratory training that are designed to increase individual and organizational effectiveness.

First, let's talk about sensitivity training as a learning technique. It's not easy to define sensitivity training; there are so many variations and labels: encounter groups, marathons, etc. And now we have a label for the genre: the human potential movement. But that's not very descriptive, either.

Chances are that the kind of sensitivity training most businessmen have been exposed to is what has been developed by the NTL (National Training Labs) Institute for Applied Behavioral Science over the past quarter century. Even so, no two NTL labs are exactly alike, which, incidentally, is one of the principal barriers to measuring the effectiveness of sensitivity training.

The basic NTL lab (now called the Human Interaction Lab) lasts for two weeks. During that time, the participant hopes to learn what impact his behavior has on others, what he does that is effective—that helps him accomplish what he wants to do—and what he does that is not effective, that gets in the way of getting things done. He also wants to understand how the behavior of others affects him, and develop the ability to express openly his feelings about the behavior of those who interact with him.

Much of the activity takes place in the T group, which consists of twelve to fifteen people and a trainer. T group sessions to a large extent are unstructured—that is, there are few planned exercises. Participants are left to their own devices to create interaction and are urged to be spontaneous in expressing what they feel at the moment. Most of the discussion is *here and now*, centered on behavior and reactions occurring within the T group. *There and then* comments, referring to behavior outside of the groups and previous to its formation, are discouraged.

With the help of the trainer, members of the group work to build trust and openness. Because the T group sessions are relatively unstructured, the trainer is absolutely necessary in creating the environment in which the participants can learn. Some samples of the kinds of comments made by participants are as follows:

"I want to tell you about something you did this morning that made me feel very good. As each of us walked into the room, you greeted us by name. You said, 'Good morning, X.' It was so personal and sincere. You seemed glad to see us."

"While I was talking, you leaned forward, and I thought you were about to get up and come over to me. I was afraid. I saw what you did as an aggressive, hostile gesture."

"I get the feeling that we are attacking X. Some of the things I hear people saying, myself included, sound so unfriendly. We are ganging up on X, and I wonder if she is just a scapegoat."

As you can see, the exchanges are highly personal, dealing with feelings rather than intellect, touching on actions and reactions that most of us avoid talking about in our day-to-day life. Yet, of course, we are affected. The behavior of others can make us happy, angry, frustrated, sad; yet we often suppress how we feel.

Sensitivity training can be a valuable, deeply moving experience. But it is *not* training. We can learn something of ourselves—how we act in certain situations, how we feel, the subterfuges we resort to in order to avoid dealing with others on an emotional level. (We don't succeed in avoiding emotions; we just think we do.)

Sensitivity training can aid in personal growth. But there are substantial reasons why, as we see it now, sensitivity training has little impact on man-in-organization:

The goal of sensitivity training is vague, seemingly oriented to getting along better with others. That's fine, but what most of us find we need are problem-solving and decision-making skills in groups. Getting along better is not enough.

The climate surrounding a sensitivity training lab tends to be artificial. Most are *stranger* groups, composed of people who have not met before and probably will never meet again. Certainly in most cases the groups are composed of people who don't have to work together. The climate of a lab is often so self-contained that the people in it cut themselves off from the outside world and become almost totally dependent on each other for the period they are together, so much so that group norms and values are of more importance to some participants than the values they hold in the outside world.

Sensitivity training is vulnerable to those participants who want to subvert the T group goals for their own purposes. Some people try to use a T group as a substitute for group therapy; others take pleasure in dominating and manipulating the T groups they attend. An alert, knowledgeable trainer can head off such "illicit" activity. But if he doesn't, most members of the group are prevented from valid learning experience.

The learning that one does in a T group is seldom reinforced and supported outside the group, either in the family or at work. Consequently there is in most people a reversion to the behavior they manifested before attending the sensitivity lab.

The executive who is considering sensitivity training for himself or for an associate must fully consider the very real risks he faces. To cite a few: the identity and credentials of the trainer may not be available to him in advance; the psychological stability of the other members of his T group cannot be assured; he may not be able to anticipate the stability of his own behavior (or that of his associate). For some, sensitivity training can be a traumatic, even disastrous, experience. People do have breakdowns in T or encounter groups. People have revelations about themselves that create a need for professional help (which may not be available). And there are people, who, because of the ineptitude of the trainer or their own personalities, experience no learning at all—it is a frustrating waste of time.

Unfortunately, the sensational aspects of sensitivity training—the casualties, the nudity (in some), the sensuality and hysteria (also in some)—have received much more publicity than the beneficial results that many people have experienced. My own feelings about sensitivity labs are best summed up in the remarks made to me recently by an experienced Organization Development professional: "I thought it did a lot for me as a person. But I would never take upon myself the responsibility for suggesting that someone else go through sensitivity training."

THE INSTRUMENTED LAB

To increase awareness of behavior and to improve interaction among people in the organization, business executives have turned more to the instrumented lab rather than to sensitivity training. For example, the Organization Development Laboratory (ODL), designed by psychologist Robert B. Morton, has as its objectives more effective group problem-solving and decision-making skills.

Before I describe the Organization Development Laboratory, a few definitions are in order. An *instrumented* lab is one in which evaluation and feedback forms are used. Samples of the forms used in Dr. Morton's ODL are reproduced in this chapter.

A *stranger* lab is one in which the participants come from different companies. They are, so far as working together, literally strangers. A *cousin* lab is held for people who work in the same company but not together. A *family* lab is for those who work together, who interact on the job.

Phase I of the ODL is usually a stranger or a cousin lab. Its objective is to help participants learn more about what goes on in the group decision-making process in terms of behavior and interaction. During the six days of Phase I, there are ten or more exercises, all simulations—that is, the work done by the D (for development) group does not *directly* relate to problems they face on the job. One exercise requires that the group rank in importance a list of factors that are said to contribute to creativity (this often reveals the tendency of many of us to try to solve a problem before the nature of the problem is clear: only a minority of D groups will start by agreeing on a definition of "creativity"). Another session involves an in-basket exercise. A third is competitive, with one or more other D groups, that demonstrates how our perception of what is happening in a situation can be influenced by changing goals: specifically doing a good job on the problem can be subordinated to the goal of "winning" over others.

After each exercise, members of the D group rate their

own performance in the group as well as the group's effectiveness (see the form, "Forces Influencing Team Effort").
Each member evaluates such issues as clarity of the group's
goals; his own expectations and the degree of fulfillment
experienced; how open he was; what kind of behavior he
saw most frequently; how the time was distributed between
discussing the nature of the goal, developing methods of
reaching the goal, and evaluating the process—the behavior and interaction.

Subsequently, the D group members will try to arrive at
a consensus evaluation of the group's activity. Usually, the
members will begin the week by giving themselves high
grades. As they progress, and learn the value of being
more objective about their effectiveness, the ratings drop,
then slowly climb again as the group coalesces and begins
to operate effectively as a team.

Name: _____ Group: _____

FORCES INFLUENCING TEAM EFFORT

1. How effective is the group? (Definition: An effective group develops when every member pushes for the most proficient resolution in the conflicts of ideas which occur when each member responsibly contributes his resources to the achievement of group goals.)

9 Most effective possible
8 Almost the most effective possible
7 Quite effective
6 Moderately effective
5 About one-half effective
4 Moderately ineffective
3 Quite ineffective
2 Almost the least effective possible and maintain a group
1 Worst possible group

Meeting#:	1	2	3	4	5	6	7
	8	9	10	11	12	13	14

2. To what extent did we talk about events arising out of our D-Group's activity (here and now), and to what extent did we talk about events which did not occur in the D-Group (there and then)?

9 Completely here and now
8 Almost completely here and now
7 Quite here and now
6 Somewhat here and now
5 Equally divided between here and now and there and then
4 Somewhat there and then
3 Quite there and then
2 Almost completely there and then
1 Completely there and then

Meeting #:	1	2	3	4	5	6	7
	8	9	10	11	12	13	14

THE ORGANIZATION DEVELOPMENT LABORATORY / © Copyright Robert B. Morton & Associates, Inc., 1969

3. To what degree were my views considered for obtaining understanding between me and the rest of the group?

9 They were completely considered, examined, evaluated and discussed in an effort to gain understanding

8 Almost completely considered, etc.

7 Considered quite a lot

6 Considered a little more than disregarded

5 Considered and disregarded about equally

4 Disregarded a little more than considered

3 Disregarded quite a bit

2 Almost completely disregarded, I was mostly tolerated

1 They were completely disregarded, I mostly plopped

0 I offered no views

Meeting #:	1	2	3	4	5	6	7
	8	9	10	11	12	13	14

4. Was I leveling with the group? That is, did I say what I really thought significant for learning, or did I find it difficult to express such ideas and feelings?

9 Completely free to express any and/or all feelings and ideas involving our interactions which I thought would contribute to learning

8 Almost completely open

7 Somewhat open

6 Slightly more open than closed

5 Neither open nor closed

4 Slightly more closed

3 Somewhat closed

2 Almost completely closed

1 Completely under wraps, closed and hidden. I had many meaningful content and process analysis ideas that I did not express

Meeting #:	1	2	3	4	5	6	7
	8	9	10	11	12	13	14

5. How clear were the group's goals in this meeting?

9 Completely clear, and explicitly stated, and agreed upon by all members

8 Almost completely clear, etc.

7 Moderately clear

6 Slightly more clear than not clear

5 Neither clear nor unclear

4 Slightly more unclear than clear

3 Moderately unclear

2 Almost completely unclear

1 Completely unclear, everyone making assumptions of each other's intentions and we don't know whether we were working to the same goal or not

Meeting#:	1	2	3	4	5	6	7
	8	9	10	11	12	13	14

5A. To what extent was time wasted.

Meeting#:	1	2	3	4	5	6	7
0/0							
	8	9	10	11	12	13	14

6. To what degree have my expectancies been achieved, neglected or violated in this meeting?

9 My expectancies have been completely achieved or satisfied

8 My expectancies have been almost completely achieved

7 My expectancies have been achieved quite a bit

6 My expectancies have been achieved only a little

5 My expectancies have been completely neglected

4 My expectancies have been violated a little

3 My expectancies have been violated quite a bit

2 My expectancies have been violated almost completely

1 My expectancies have been violated completely

Meeting#:	1	2	3	4	5	6	7
	8	9	10	11	12	13	14

7. Content — Process — Methodology Orientation
Per cent Distribution

Meeting #	1	2	3	4	5	6	7	8	9	10	11	12	13	14
1 Content														
2 Process														
3 Methodology														

8. Group Atmosphere Words: (Check on the adjoining sheet as many words as needed to describe your development group session).

	1	2	3	4	5	6	7	8	9	10	11	12	13	14
10 Productive														
9 Rewarding														
8 Opinionated														
7 Ineffective														
6 Competitive														
5 Evasive														
4 Work														
3 Fight														
2 Flight														
1 Tense														
Meeting #														

9. Change Agent Skills.

A. Group Task Functions:

	1	2	3	4	5	6	7	8	9	10	11	12	13	14
10 Developing Superordinate Goals														
9 Confronting Issues														
8 Data Seeking														
7 Identifying Alternatives														
6 Integrating Divergent Ideas														
5 Evaluating														
4 Dominating														
3 Testing for Feasibility														
2 Keeping Group on Goals														
1 Initiating														

Meeting #

B. Group Maintenance Functions:

	1	2	3	4	5	6	7	8	9	10	11	12	13	14
10 Gate Keeping														
9 Giving Support														
8 Process Analyzing														
7 Listening														
6 Providing Information														
5 Clarifying Positions														
4 Following														
3 Blocking														
2 Providing Methodology														
1 Risk Taking for Significant Issues														

Meeting #

At the end of the week, each D group member is asked to rate himself on behavior that influences effectiveness. Then he rates his fellow members. The respective ratings are passed around the table, and all the participants talk about the ratings they have made. (See the "Behavior which Influences Team and Individual Effectiveness" forms and explanation starting on page 108.)

BEHAVIOR WHICH INFLUENCES TEAM AND INDIVIDUAL EFFECTIVENESS

INSTRUCTIONS: Read the description of each of the variables. Each step 9 to 1 represents a gradation between the descriptive references. Read the description here before scaling the variable. Scale all persons on each variable before moving to the next variable.

1. INITIATES: This scale measures degrees of initiating activity. Nine (9) represents behavior that is forceful and frequent in the initiating of new ideas and actions and pushing in some direction. Four (4) represents behavior of some initiating, mostly following and committed to actions

group goals by going astray, pushing personal goals not integrated into group goals or leading the group in the wrong direction.

4. EVALUATES: Behavior is evaluated against explicit specified standards related to the task or more abstract standards. Nine (9), behavior, ideas and accomplishments are evaluated against identified and agreed upon goals. At mid-point (5) evaluation is based upon the practicality of how "it works." One (1) represents the behavior of evaluating on such abstractness as "good" or "bad" or "that's the way we've always done it."

5. CONFLICT OF IDEAS: This scale measures to the degree that the person initiates, engages in the exchange of conflicting ideas in an attempt to sharpen the learning or behaves in such a way as to suppress conflict of ideas. Nine (9) represents the active promotion of the exchange of ideas in order to sharpen the issues. Six (6) to (5) represents the avoidance of conflict, whereas (4) to (3) involves cooling the situation and (2) represents actively retarding or suppressing the expression of conflicting ideas. One (1) represents be-

represents minimal involvement and/or commitment.

2. FACILITATES: This scale measures the degree new inputs are facilitated (9) or hindered (1). Nine (9) represents a very high level of encouraging, facilitating and supporting others in presenting new ideas, procedures, goals, etc. From (6) to (4) behavior is primarily supportive for new ideas, etc., which are within the range of being personally acceptable. Two (2) or (1) indicate blocking of ideas, etc., which are not acceptable — "Not Invented Here" (NIH) behavior.

3. GOAL DIRECTED: This measures the degree behavior is directed by group goals or personal goals. Nine (9) represents behavior which is directed to identifying the goals which are influencing behavior, helping to clarify and progress in a group goal directed manner. Four (4) represents lack of attention to over-all goals and directions and (1) is the extreme of disregarding

of immature personalities and should be avoided.

6. SUPPORTS OTHERS: This variable measures the degree a person extends or withholds support. Nine (9) indicates you consider the person as actively giving support by encouraging, etc. Seven (7) indicates giving support to someone else carrying the ball. Five (5) indicates support if others are responsible. Three (3) indicates a willingness to support if no commitment is required. One (1) represents a withholding of support or encouragement.

7. EXPRESSES FEELINGS: This variable measures the degrees the person being rated expresses or denies his and other's feelings. Nine (9) indicates the practice of expressing feelings openly regarding any issue or persons. Seven (7) supports others. Five (5) indicates caution and restraint. Four (4) suppresses one's feelings, and (3) restrains others. One (1) indicates denial of feelings.

THE ORGANIZATION DEVELOPMENT LABORATORY / © *Copyright Robert B. Morton & Associates, Inc. 1969*

8. LEVELS: This scale measures the degree of leveling. Nine (9) represents confronting the critical issues through leveling. Seven (7) he levels quite a bit. Five (5) represents guarded use of leveling. Three (3) indicates degrees of avoidance and (1) blocking others from leveling.

9. CONFRONTS: This scale tests the degree the person confronts issues and people. Nine (9) indicates behavior which brings the issues into the open. Seven (7) confronts when avoiding of conflict is possible. Three (3) actively avoids confronting by glossing over issues. One (1) indicates behavior which either denies issues, politely disregards, or talks about them in a general, theoretical way using remote illustrations rather than "here and now" behavior. Positions seven (7) to four (4) represent progressively reducing degrees of confrontation.

10. DECISION MAKING: This scale rates the definiteness of decision making. Nine (9) represents a decision making process through openly considering the significant alternatives and letting others know where

one stands. Six (6) to four (4) rates as superficially or minimally considering the alternatives and taking strong positions. One (1) indicates tendency to get lost in words, small details and unspoken assumptions, leaving others unsure where he stands.

11. SEEKS RECOGNITION: This scale examines the manner recognition is achieved. Nine (9) represents seeking recognition for its own sake beyond regard of legitimacy. Seven (7) legitimate recognition is openly sought and accepted. Five (5) minimizes value to himself and (3) avoids or is embarrassed. One (1) is a denial of valid feelings.

12. DOMINATES: This scale varies from dominating to acquiescing. Nine (9) indicates behavior that dominates the group on the basis of status or power. Five (5) represents controlling or leading in congruence or group goal achievement. One (1) indicates submitting or following the control of others

Name: _____

Group: _____

BEHAVIOR WHICH INFLUENCES TEAM AND INDIVIDUAL EFFECTIVENESS

RATING SHEETS

INSTRUCTIONS: Make a circle indicating how you rate the individual you are rating. It is best to rate all persons on one item first before moving to the second item for any one person. If you cannot rate a person on a scale, omit that scale.

1. INITIATES IDEAS, ETC.:

Initiates' and drives toward own ideas, etc.		Mostly initiating, but permits others' ideas with moderate or variable commitment and support.			Some initiating, but mostly waiting for others and providing support.			Minimal initiating, involvement or commitment to action or giving of support.	
9	8	7	6	5	4	3	2	1

THE ORGANIZATION DEVELOPMENT LABORATORY / © Copyright Robert B. Morton & Associates, Inc. 1969

2. FACILITATES NEW IDEAS:

9	8	7	6	5	4	3	2	1
Actively facilitates introduction of new ideas, information, and input from others regardless of his level of agreement.		Supports the introduction of new ideas, if plausible.		Supports or maintains ideas or input with which he concurs.		Is indifferent to new ideas or new approaches.		Actively hinders introduction of new ideas. "NIH, yes! but we've tried that before" behavior.

3. GOAL DIRECTED:

9	8	7	6	5	4	3	2	1
Helps to identify, clarify, establish validity and keep group on its goals.		Mostly stays with central goals and helps to keep group goal oriented.		Often misses the principal direction or topic and becomes involved in "short term" or divergent issues.		Often to frequently pursues own goals and leads the group away from its goal orientation.	

4. EVALUATES:

Evaluates activities in relation to levels of achievement and progress toward identified goals.	Evaluates in terms of questions of short term practicality and logic.	Evaluates in terms of unrevealed personalized values.	Evaluates in terms of undefined or generalized standards of "good or bad." Assumes if others are not "against" they are "for."

9	8	7	6	5	4	3	2	1
Promotes conflict of ideas to sharpen issues by bringing up or supporting relevant, controversial issues.		Engages in and supports conflicts of ideas.	Avoids conflict of ideas, if possible, otherwise disengages himself.		Cools, pushes for politeness, or otherwise dulls the sharpness of ideas in conflict.		Aggressively retards or suppresses the conflict of ideas.	Sees conflict as personality clashes and/or immature behavior.

6. SUPPORTS OTHERS:

9	8	7	6	5	4	3	2	1
Takes responsibility for encouraging others in what they are trying to do.		Gives support when others share responsibility.	Gives support when others are responsible.			Supports if not required to commit himself to follow through.		Withholds support. Risks little for others.

7. EXPRESSES FEELINGS:

9	8	7	6	5	4	3	2	1
Expresses openly feelings regarding issues and persons.		Supports others to express feelings.		Restrained in expressing feelings.	Keeps own feelings to himself.	Restrains others from expressing feelings.		Denies presence or importance of feelings.

8. LEVELS:

9	8	7	6	5	4	3	2	1
Freely expresses himself regarding the most significant current issues.	Levels quite a bit.		Expresses himself guardedly regarding significant issues in the group.			Avoids talking about pressing issues.	Blocks others from leveling.	

9. CONFRONTS:

9	8	7	6	5	4	3	2	1
Confronts any significant issue regarding group effort and how the group works.	Confronts issues which do not threaten group.		Confronts issues which have prior approval.			Avoids issues, actively pursues being a peacemaker.	Either denies the significant issues or talks about them so "there and then" or in such broad generalities as not to confront the "here and now" persons or issues.	

10. DECISION MAKING:

Makes decisions by openly evaluating alternatives and taking a revealed position.	Superficially considers some available alternatives and takes strong position.	Decisions get lost in generalities and unspoken assumptions. You don't know where he stands.

11. SEEKS RECOGNITION:

9	8	7	6	5	4	3	2	1
Seeks recognition to a degree that annoys others.		Sees that legitimate recognition is received.		Politely minimizes efforts by others to express legitimate recognition.		Avoids legitimate recognition.		Denies validity. "Oh, there was nothing to it," false humility.

12. DOMINATES:

9	8	7	6	5	4	3	2	1
Dominates group on basis of status or personal aggrandizement.		Dominates on basis of habit or group acquiescence.		Dominates on basis of group acceptance for team achievement.		Avoids dominating but exerts influence for group direction.	Reticent in dealing with issues.	Acquiesces to others' control.

Finally, a participant's self-rating is combined with the ratings of others on a summary sheet, from which a profile emerges.

Name: _____

Group: _____

BEHAVIOR WHICH INFLUENCES TEAM AND INDIVIDUAL EFFECTIVENESS

DATA SUMMARY SHEET

Respondents

Group Roles:	Self	1	2	3	4	5	6	7	8	9
1. Initiates Ideas, Actions or Procedures										
2. Facilitates Introduction of New Ideas and Information										
3. Goal Directed										

4. Evaluates							
5. Conflict of Ideas							
6. Supports Others							
7. Expresses Feelings							
8. Levels							
9. Confronts Issues							
10. Decision Making							
11. Seeks Recognition							
12. Dominates							

THE ORGANIZATION DEVELOPMENT LABORATORY / © *Copyright Robert B. Morton & Associates, Inc. 1969*

CONFRONTING THE REAL ISSUES

Phase II, which also lasts six days, is a team-building or family lab. From the outset, participants work on some of the problems that cause them trouble on the job. The first task of the groups is to ask the question, "What can I (we) do to be more effective on the job?"

Of course, this question can be translated any number of ways. For example, "What are we doing now that we probably should not be doing or should be doing differently?" Or, "What should we do more of or do better?" The avoidance mechanisms usually swing into high gear.

In one lab I observed, some participants wound up blaming other people for their troubles. ("If those jerks wouldn't foul us up, we'd have no problems.") Others came to the conclusion, "This problem is bigger than all of us," which, of course, put the blame on the "system" or the home office. In making one choice or the other, people were searching for ways *not* to confront the real issue: There were things they were doing or not doing that caused them to be less than effective in getting the results they wanted from their work.

There were, however, some managers present who recognized what was happening (even more, what was not happening) and who persisted in asking: "What can *we* do?"

At that point, another familiar avoidance technique came into play: a preoccupation with causes. For example, supervisor Jerry Dunphy has a recurring problem with his counterpart in another department, Ted Wilson. Wilson's operation sometimes must be called upon to complete work originating with Dunphy's group. Most of the orders are custom, and periodically Dunphy must send the work in progress over to Wilson for a particular process.

When the goods are sent over with an improper work order, Wilson sends them back, a step that often delays completion of the order for two or three days. On one occasion, a proper work order was sent the second time around, but there was a typo in the instructions. Again, Wilson sent everything back to Dunphy.

A group can get awfully involved with what causes such behavior—so involved, in fact, that the problem is simply diagnosed or analyzed. It doesn't get solved.

Therefore, the question has to be asked: *Considering what we are doing that causes us problems, what alternative actions or behavior would be more effective?* This, of course, is quite different from getting mired in causality, which often turns into an academic exercise. Asking "Who or what specifically is responsible for this mess?" (Dunphy or Wilson?) is not as helpful as asking, "What would we rather do or see done?" Here the members of the group are charged with the necessity of defining actions and behavior that, to the best of their knowledge, would be more effective.

(This is not to say that looking for causes is always wrong. But even if the cause is known, a problem is not solved until action is taken.)

Another question: *What do we need to do to achieve the alternatives we have chosen?* In most cases, there are people, knowledge, and structure that have to be changed, acquired, or removed.

A third avoidance technique these managers resorted to —one frequently observed in problem-solving groups—is the failure to assign responsibility and to schedule a timetable for implementing the solution. Once a group has come up with recommendations for action or an action plan, a surprising number of its members seem content to adjourn without pinning down who is responsible for seeing that the plan is carried out. Nor do they set up a time period within which the job is to be done.

So members of the D group have to be gently persuaded to deal with these questions: *Who is responsible for seeing that these actions are taken? What kind of a timetable are we working within?* Does every member of the group know these "who" and "when" answers?

It takes a lot of patience and persistence to confront and solve problems—and quite a bit of understanding, especially on the manager's part. He has to accept the probability that nearly everyone will do a certain amount of ducking and weaving before admitting even partial responsibility for the troublesome situation.

Usually Phase II participants have to be persuaded to confront the issues. It's natural to want to avoid them, especially if that's what people have been doing on the job. And behavior in a team-building lab will often mirror on-the-job behavior.

After each of the Phase II laboratory sessions, participants use the same rating forms they employed in the Phase I lab; and at the end of the week, there is the leveling that closed out the first week.

A SIMULATION TO BUILD THE TEAM

Most people find laboratory learning exciting. You can actually see yourself making progress. It is painful. No one really likes to confront unpleasant issues. It is effective. You have a goal to achieve, and you can readily relate what you are doing in the lab to the objective you—and the group—want to achieve.

There is no question that laboratory learning contributes mightily to the building of effective group behavior. That's why the laboratory can be beneficial to the participants in a task force if only so they understand *process*. It can be helpful for them to be able to answer these questions at any point in the life of the task force: What's going on here? What kind of behavior are we seeing? What influence is it having on our interaction with each other, our effectiveness? What behavior would help the group better?

Before the task force begins its work, the members could undergo a team-building exercise, perhaps three days of simulations. In most cases, a minimum of three days of interaction is necessary for a group to coalesce, for the members to think of themselves as a group, to put the group's objectives over those of the individuals comprising it. Simulated exercises are recommended, so that the group can concentrate on the process, on building effective interaction, not on trying to work on real problems (until the group is effective as a group).

Ideally, for the simulation phase and for the initial, problem-solving sessions that parallel a Phase II lab, the task force should have as a resource a *facilitator*. He acts as a trainer in a laboratory group. He is a man well versed in small-group behavior and in techniques of intervention to explain what goes on in order to help the group be more effective.

The facilitator should be available to the task force during its life to play the role of observer, to intervene when the group feels it is necessary, and to arrange refresher simulations when the group feels it needs to back off from the real problems to collect more data about its own ways of operating.

I want to stress that laboratory training, team-building simulations, and the facilitator, while desirable, are not essential. Task forces can be and are successful without them. Nevertheless, such training and assistance often speed effectiveness and deepen the awareness of task force members of the behavior that contributes most to getting a job done well.

What we shall now consider are leadership roles in the group, shaping effective group behavior, and dealing with obstructive behavior. Of course, no manager should take upon himself the role of psychiatrist in leading a group. He cannot hope to know the attitudes and motivations of the members of the group he leads. He is concerned with their behavior, with helping them be effective with each other, in attaining the goals of the group.

SEVEN

FORMING THE TASK FORCE

Who should sit on a task force? How large should it be? Are there jobs a task force shouldn't be asked to handle?

These are questions that invariably arise in any consideration of a team approach to problem-solving and decision-making. There are few hard-and-fast guidelines. But, in the spirit of all-generalizations-are-false-including-this-one, let me try to formulate some broad recommendations.

How large should a task force be?

The size usually depends on what kind of a job is to be done, how many corporate functions are involved, and how many kinds of expertise are needed. In most cases, eight, possibly up to ten, constitute a reasonable maximum. The constraints that have to be considered are: optimum interaction between participants, number of individual schedules to be coordinated, and the expense of taking key people from their regular jobs, even on a part-time basis.

American Airlines recently had as few as four top executives working on a definition of the union lead function. The lead man, although a union member, provides on-the-job training and work group scheduling. The union has in the past set up criteria to determine who should be a lead man and with what authority he should operate. However, in the latest contract negotiations, the union asked management to establish criteria which, upon union acceptance, would become part of the new contract. Considering the complex nature of the problem and the knowledge and authority needed to resolve it, the American task force, though small, was quite sufficient.

At the other end of the scale, twelve supervisors at an American station formed a task force to work out problems between ramp service and passenger service functions. Such a large group might be unwieldy except for these factors: all of the supervisors knew each other; there were only two functions involved; and the problem was somewhat restricted. This task force, incidentally, extended its activity beyond interface problems to collaborate successfully on the preparation of a new safety manual to augment what the airline supplied.

There is, in making up the task force, a temptation to bring in as many resources as possible. But, of course, as the group becomes larger and harder to coalesce, the point of diminishing returns will be reached. A preferable approach, when many kinds of expertise are involved, is to follow the ADQ example (see Chapter Three) and distribute responsibilities for those areas among a few. Each member of the task force, therefore, becomes a link with several experts, whose contributions can be made through him or before the entire group on a summons basis.

What kind of people should be chosen for a task force?
The best qualification for a member of a task force is that he cannot be spared from his regular duties. So pick the man who is indispensable.

Recently, the director of organization development in one large New York-based firm set about forming his first task force. The objective was a major one, and he had top management's backing. Unfortunately, he did a poor job of selling the task force to the departments involved. They sent him second- and third-string people, individuals who could easily be spared. They did a respectable job for him. But because the task force members were known to be people of lesser importance, the team lacked the prestige and authority it should have had.

Therefore, the best recommendation is to make every effort to get the most knowledgeable and best-known people you can.

Second, try to get people who interact well. That does not mean homogeneity. Too many people in a group who think the same way can spell trouble. By "think the same way" I mean they tend to approach a discussion similarly— their *methods* of thinking are alike. What is recommended is that you mix people who are as follows:

Analytical. They have the ability to diagnose the causes of a problem, to pull pieces of a situation apart so that they can be examined more easily. These are the "why" people.

Judgmental. They evaluate, test, and measure the practicality of an idea and are able to foresee the direct and indirect consequences of its application.

Creative. People who think associatively are those we usually term creative. They see links and connections between ideas that other people simply don't see. This skill is, contrary to popular mythology, the result of training rather than heredity.

All three types of ratiocination are vital in solving a problem, and, if it's possible, a task force should be formed incorporating all three.

Third, task force members should be somewhat influential outside the group. One international airline formed a task force with the objective of recommending how women could be utilized more effectively as specialists and managers in an organization dominated by men. The task force was made up largely of women. One important factor had been overlooked: If women were to be accorded equal opportunity, the men who dominated the organization had to be persuaded to provide the opportunity. There should have been a number of men on the task force who understood the persuasion problem as well as the discrimination and could help direct the team's efforts to this end, and who, by their very presence on the task force, could have rendered some influence themselves. It may sound male chauvinistic, but the male representation could prevent the task force from becoming an academic exercise.

One note of caution: Try to avoid the "perceived expert" effect. Sometimes in forming a group management will appoint one man whose knowledge or authority is recognized by others as so superior to theirs that the group will have a difficult time in achieving the wide-open participation that is necessary to its success. The best recommendations are: first, balance the expertness of one with varied expertness of several, and second, don't play up to excess the credentials of any one member.

A variation of the perceived expert effect can be created by a "resident authority" on the task force—that is, the members of the group are fairly equal in status, except for one or two representatives from higher management. Their presence can intimidate the others and prevent democratic interaction within the group. It must be made clear that these higher managers are not to exercise their greater authority in the group. To offset this risk, some companies aim for a representation that cuts diagonally through the management levels. Not only is the makeup interdepartmental, but the authority present is sufficiently within a range that does not permit a radical differentiation in power.

Are there tasks that shouldn't be assigned to a team?
Yes. There are at least two conditions under which a group can be expected to be less efficient than individuals:

1. When time is a factor and an early decision is required. Short deadlines tend to keep the group from warming up properly, from opening up, from building the trust necessary to collaboration. The greatest dangers, in a pressure atmosphere, are that the leadership will become autocratic, or that the first solution that even *sounds* feasible will be adopted without sufficient evidence, or that the group will be so paralyzed by the time pressure that nothing will happen.

Consensus is the strength of the task force approach—but it takes time to achieve it.

2. When problems can best be solved by quantitative methods that eliminate or reduce narrowly the opportunities for qualitative analysis or speculation, groups tend to

be less effective than individuals. Some examples are: defective shipments received due to packaging failures, manufacturing equipment failures due to malfunctions, sales territory allocations by prospect potential.

Such problems, too, lend themselves to departmental resolution. Seldom do they require interdepartmental expertise.

What determines whether a task force should operate on a full-time or a part-time basis?

There are, of course, the obvious factors such as time pressure (how quickly the matter has to be resolved) and availability of resources (the extent to which key people can be away from their regularly assigned duties).

But there are less obvious, more complex considerations. For example, although it is probable that the organization of the future will accommodate many full-time task forces or project teams, the corporate structure of today will undoubtedly exist more comfortably with part-time groups. The objective, after all, is not to disrupt operations but to maximize resources already available. For an organization that is yet more identified with the traditional authoritarian model, that is not extensively decentralized, to attempt an overnight transition to temporary, autonomous teams could mean more than disruption. It could be disastrous.

Furthermore, crash efforts that often seem to justify full-time task forces allow less time to build collaborative interaction with the regularly constituted functions of the organization. Those managers not sitting on the team may be slow in accepting its mandate and authority. A deliberate pace, a certain tact, can lay the groundwork for collaboration that a sudden fiat, or fait accompli, cannot. On the side of the task force, time is needed to test its tentative solutions, to obtain as much feedback as possible from every function involved in the objective of the group, even though those corporate functions are not directly represented.

The ADQ task force described in Chapter Three is an example of a full-time group that has taken the time and exercised the diplomacy necessary to build collaboration and get acceptance and feedback. Even so, there is always the danger, in the average organization today, that a high-priority, full-time task force will be regarded by others with suspicion, and that their functions and even their motives will be questioned.

These are not arguments against full-time teams. However, these are the kinds of problems an executive must consider in setting up a task force.

How much autonomy should a task force have?

The task force should have a clear track to reach its objective. There will often be, however, pressures from the outside that can obstruct its progress. There may be managers who refuse to recognize and collaborate with the team. Others will try to unduly influence the group's work.

While it is true that no task force can operate with complete autonomy—as, indeed, no functional group can —nevertheless it may require a protector, one who can, through high-level negotiations, enhance its acceptance, and, as a last resort, can enforce cooperation (which is not the same and is not as effective as collaboration).

But chiefly the executive "umbrella" exists to provide the proportionate authority necessary during the life of the task force as the group redefines the problem it faces and selects whatever new objectives emerge from its work. It is not enough for management to say, "Establish the limitations of the task force at the outset so that there can be no question of its areas of operation and its constraints." The operating areas and constraints can be expected to change as the work progresses. And these changes are authorized by the high-level executive who is monitoring the task force.

Can a task force be permanent?

Not by the definition we use today. Task forces are temporary, task-oriented groups whose function is to solve problems, make decisions, and exploit opportunities that cannot be effectively dealt with by regularly constituted departments or divisions.

In future organizations, such as Likert's System 4 model, there may be a permanent matrix for groups, although the groups themselves and their relationships with each other may change as the need changes.

Can employees on their own initiative form interdepartmental, interdisciplinary teams?

The initiative may come from the would-be task force members, but the justification and authority, in most organizations today, must come from above. Bear in mind that task forces, to be effective, must bear responsibility for their recommendations. They are not simply to petition or to advise.

In my opinion, management would be very short-sighted indeed to overlook or discourage such initiative. One of the major problems a manager today can create for himself is to try to operate against the informal groups that are to be found in nearly every organization. People will form such groups. It's safe to say they belong in close associations. At least it is an apparent need. So such initiative should be considered seriously and authorized wherever there is the slightest justification.

Most of the constraints on a task force's operation derive from the organization with which we are most familiar today. We may be—and I believe indeed we are—heading

TASK FORCE MGMT

(1) DEFINITION

(2) FORMING THE TF
   (1) size
   (2) kind of people

(3) CHARACTERISTICS OF TF
   (1) OP. RESP.
   (2) INTERDEPT.
   (3) INTER DISIPLINARY
   (4) AUTONOMY IS HIGH
   (5) DECISION BY "CONSENSUS"

(4) GOOD PTS

(5) BAD PTS

(6) TF SHOULD
   CONCENTRATE ON ...

toward a more decentralized, organic corporate body in which the vital work will be conducted by groups that are flexible and ever shifting in emphasis, objectives, and authority. But the realities we recognize at the present time necessitate the operation of task forces with certain "givens." The exciting potential of the task force is in its ability, through extensive application, to change those realities.

Of course, those realities will require a different perspective on what we define as management. In the next chapter we'll take a look at some of those new leadership requirements.

EIGHT

LEADERSHIP IN A TASK FORCE

"The better job I do as a manager," an experienced executive said to me recently, "the duller it gets." His description of the manager's dilemma is accurate. If the manager does his job as most management literature tells him to, he will delegate most of his authority, develop competent people who could step into his shoes on short notice, religiously abstain from doing any work that subordinates could and should do, and bring employees into as many decisions as possible. Thus, the more successful he is in managing, the less the content—the specific duties—of his job. Of course, he should be "borrowing" as much of his boss's job as possible. But not every boss is dedicated to helping subordinate managers enrich their jobs. Too, the higher jobs become more general and less divisible.

Thus the capable manager gets rid of as many duties as he can. Unfortunately, he may find that, because of the rigidity of the organization chart or the unwillingness of his boss, he is not permitted to enlarge his area of responsibility. He will probably find, too, that he has limited freedom to innovate. So he marks time and fights boredom as well as he can until a promotion comes his way.

In this chapter, we shall discuss leadership less in the old-fashioned terms of content and more in the newer sense as process management—the manager as facilitator, as a resource to the people who work for and with him. Those are roles that managers increasingly will perform, as the organization chart abandons the tight little boxes and the solid black lines, and as managers acquire and surrender responsibility for temporary, fast-changing work groups. Whether the manager is in fact the most knowledgeable, competent, experienced member of his work group will not be important, for his primary roles will be to find new opportunities to challenge his associates, to maintain a creative climate in which they can invest *their* expertise and experience.

Tomorrow's executive will be a manager of *process*. Either as leader or member of a task force, his function will be to facilitate a productive interaction between its members.

SELECTION OF A LEADER

Just as the traditional role of the manager will change, so will the method of selection of a group leader. Of course, a team director can be chosen on the basis of authority— he has by virtue of his regular position more authority than anyone else on the task force. But amount of authority should not be the primary criterion, even in most cases. There may be times when, to give a group more power and prestige, its leader should be an executive high enough in the hierarchy to insure that the task force work is accepted and implemented. However, the same result can generally be achieved if the executive to whom the task force reports (but who is not a member of the group) is on one of the higher tiers.

The authority, power, and influence of the leader should have no internal significance for the task force. Often the less he tries to bring into the group, the better he—and everyone else—performs.

In addition to authority, there are at least four other ways to select a task force leader. One is tap the man whose initiative and efforts have resulted in the formation of the group—the man who first defined the problem or brought the challenge to higher management's attention. Or looking at it from the other direction, the man chosen is the one who will be heading up a permanent group to continue the implementation after the task force has phased out. A third criterion derives from the operational area most involved in the task force's objective. For example, if the goal is a new product development, even though R&D, engineering, sales production, finance, etc., are all involved, the group leader might be a marketing manager.

The fourth method of selection is easily the most intriguing: Let the task force choose its own leader. At the same time, the group will usually let it be known what it expects of a leader: how formal his leadership will be, how much personal authority he will be called upon to wield, etc. Or, indeed, the mantle might be passed around, as in the example of the Research Institute task force (see Chapter Three).

Group selection of a leader should take place toward the end of the team-building exercise that was recommended in Chapter Six. For most effective results, leader designation should be by consensus, not by majority vote.

It will sometimes happen that, during the life of a task force, the leader who was appointed by management or chosen by the group will prove ineffective or, because of illness, termination, etc., will have to be replaced. Regardless of how *he* was appointed, his successor should, in most cases, be recommended (and, if possible, chosen) by the group (again, if possible, he should be from the group).

What should be looked for in a task force leader? Aside from technical and managerial qualifications, he should be experienced in process, with proven ability to function effectively as part of a group, and have as one personal goal the wish to help the task force successfully accomplish its objectives. Putting this last point more bluntly, he needs the satisfaction of success, and he likes the applause.

HIS OUTSIDE ROLES

While this chapter will concern itself chiefly with leadership roles in the group sessions—that's where most of the interaction takes place and where the team's effectiveness is built—nevertheless the leader does have vital roles to play outside meetings, roles that should also be considered in selecting the man who will lead the task force. For example:

• *Linking pin.* In a team-oriented organization, the task force leader will probably be a member of one or more other teams, and it is likely that some of the work his group does relates to tasks of those other teams. His will be the job of establishing and maintaining collaboration between the task force he leads and the other related groups in which he participates. Certainly he will be the team's link with higher management groups. (If his is the only task force operating, he maintains liaison with regularly assigned managers whose departments are affected by his group's task.) The concept I am advancing here is based on Likert's System 4 organization, which is composed almost entirely of overlapping and related groups. His role as linking pin is to provide coordination between groups and access to the power centers.

• *Protector*. This, of course, is a traditional role of the manager, but one that is often unfortunately given short shrift. In the life of nearly every task force, there will be intergroup conflicts: toes of those outside the task force will be stepped on and boundaries of other departments will be crossed as the team pursues its objectives. Inevitably there will be those who feel that the task force has been given too much authority, that its authority overlaps the jurisdiction of regular managers. The team leader, therefore, will have to soothe ruffled feathers, explain team functions to those who are not participating, and serve as a buffer. Whatever suspicion, complaints, or anger are aroused by the activities of the task force, it is the leader who must bear the brunt. He must not permit the comments and actions of those outside the task force to impede its effectiveness. He must keep communications open between the task force and "outsiders," and at the same time insist that those communications be directed *through* him.

• *Clearinghouse for all task force operations*. Much of the work of the group will be conducted between meetings, and the leader must insure that all extra-meeting work be cleared with him. He must be apprised of all problems, progress, and needs that arise between task force group sessions.

• *Negotiator and evaluator.* His manpower needs usually have to be worked out with the permanent managers of task force personnel. Conflicts in schedules, priorities, and duties will inevitably arise, and are settled through negotiations with the managers concerned. And, as has already been stated, the task force leader evaluates the performance of group members for the benefit of their regular managers.

HIS INSIDE ROLES

In meetings of the task force, the leader encourages and supports helpful group behavior (see Chapter Nine) and discourages obstructive behavior (see Chapter Ten). He must set the tone for the meetings, the atmosphere in which team members can function at an optimum. There are few guidelines. But, such as they are, we shall examine some roles he should not play, and others no one can play as well as he.

First, on the negative side, he must be careful not to lean over so far to be democratic that he creates a leadership vacuum. It is acceptable for him to think of himself as *primus inter pares,* but he should retain enough primacy to avoid interminable and unproductive meetings, to help resolve personality conflicts, to cut off destructive competition for his leadership, and to insure that the resources of the group are effectively tapped.

On the other hand, he must be careful not to exert so much primacy that he forces the group's deliberations toward a predetermined objective in a predetermined period of time. He is a facilitator, not a dictator. He provides some of the tools that a task force needs to get its work done. He does not become a tool of the group, nor does the group become his tool.

The positive, formal roles he should play in meetings follow. He should:

1. *State the problem.* This is anything but easy. Very often it is the group that defines the real problem. What is originally given to it to solve may not, in fact, be the work it eventually winds up doing. Thus care must be taken to state the general nature of the problem, not define it for the group and so unnecessarily limit the range of its exploration. Let's take an example: Company X manufactures on the East Coast and ships to the West Coast market. The company currently is taking a price beating from local West Coast suppliers. What is the real problem? It is *not* how to get X's products to the West Coast at a price comparable to that charged by local competition. Rather, what has to be resolved is this: How can X sell competitively on the West Coast?

The task force solution may be to set up manufacturing facilities in California, or find alternate ways to ship, or manufacture parts in the East and assemble in the West, or stress the superior quality and application at the higher price—and on and on.

Too often the problem is stated in such a way that the range of solutions is unwittingly limited, or the group starts to resolve the wrong problem. Therefore, the most general nature of the problem is put before the group, and the actual definition of the problem and the parameters are left to the task force.

Of course, there usually are limitations imposed on the group. Company X assigns its task force the responsibility of finding a solution that does not necessitate any capital expenditure in excess of five hundred thousand dollars. Such limitations should be spelled out before the group begin deliberations. If possible, the limitations should not be absolute. Using Company X again, if savings could be achieved that matched the expenditure, would the company be willing to make the investment?

It's safe to say that most limitations are really relative; they are subject to re-examination and change in the light of task force research.

In stating the problem, the leader must also be careful not to reveal which direction *he* would like the discussions to take. If he personally has a vested interest, he should assign the definition role to a member who hasn't such an interest.

2. *Restate the problem*. This is a necessary function, especially since the problem may change in definition. The leader should make sure that everyone understands the meaning of each person's contribution in terms of what is to be accomplished by the group as a whole. And when one member proposes an idea or solution, the leader's job is to test the understanding of all the members: Do they clearly understand what has been proposed?

One of the most annoying features of a group discussion is repetition. People make suggestions without seeming to realize that those suggestions have already been made. Participants criticize a proposal that has already successfully withstood that same criticism. The problem is that people do not listen, usually because they are concentrating on what they will say. So the progress of a group toward its goals depends in large part on how successfully a leader can cut down on the repetition of others by a judicious bit of repetition himself.

Also, each possible solution proposed by task force members has to be evaluated against the problem and against the various constraints such as time limits, available resources, feasibility, cost, etc.

3. *Encourage alternatives.* Almost any group that is charged with coming up with ideas and solutions runs the risk of settling on one of those solutions before others can be proposed. This is why groups are really much better at evaluating solutions that have already been submitted than in originating them. It is therefore up to the leader to see that no possible solution or contribution is stifled, that no participant is "going along" because he hesitates to express his disagreement or his lack of understanding of what has been discussed.

One technique that encourages contributions from members calls for each person to write his idea on a blackboard or chart. No discussion of any idea is permitted until *all* have been recorded, the one exception being a question to clear up misunderstanding. It is essential that the leader enforce this rule: There is to be no evaluation until all contributions are recorded. This technique can be repeated during a session and at every session until the group members themselves become sufficiently supportive as to insist on their own that every contribution be entertained, that no one be shut off or blocked.

4. *Keep the discussion relevant.* Nothing kills the effectiveness of a meeting more than the group's willingness to let the discussion wander all over the subject and away from it. The leader must know when to channel the talk back to the subject, which in itself involves considerable risk: He has to decide what is relevant and what is not.

Other members of the group may not agree with his decision. Still, the leader must take that risk, because often members of a group will be hesitant to question the relevance of the comments of other members.

However, when the leader challenges a member as not being relevant, he should extend to the member the opportunity to relate what he is saying to the objective of the meeting. And when the leader senses he may be unfair to a member, he can always pose this question to the group as a whole: "Does anyone else here share my feeling that what he is saying takes us away from the goal?" Often a question such as that will elicit support that otherwise was not evident.

A chairman has to be especially wary of the contribution that invites digression by the way it is stated: the wrong terminology, too many qualifications that arouse objections, two or three premises in one statement. Also, a man may make an observation that is valid and to the point, but in making it may refer to something else that is not to the point. That someone else will pick up the stray thread and pursue it can be counted on, and that's when the leader has to step in, restate the contribution correctly, and eliminate the irrelevancy.

5. *Summarize.* This is a matter of timing—too early, and the summary may forestall further contributions; too late, and the discussion may already have become unfocused or chaotic (and unsummarizable). The leader should decide whether it is time for a summary of the points made thus far, but, again, he will probably find it helpful to get the group's agreement that his summary does, in fact, cover the necessary ground. Furthermore, he should be sure that the data he has rejected in his summary the group also considers irrelevant or unhelpful.

A form of summarizing that is frequently helpful is *testing assumptions*. Let's return to the example of Company X, engaged in price competition on the West Coast. The chairman notes that much of the conversation has centered on warehouse facilities on the West Coast that will permit a slower and less expensive form of shipping from the East Coast. Nothing firm has been established, and so the leader steps in with an opener like this: "We seem to be operating on certain assumptions. As I understand it, many of you seem to favor setting up warehouses in certain coastal locations and . . ."

This kind of minor summary can help sharpen the focus of the discussion, or it may, by throwing the assumptions into relief, elicit opposition from those members who hadn't been aware that the discussion had gone so far as to imply solutions such as warehousing.

6. *Insist on feedback on the tentative solution.* When the group appears to have settled on a solution, the leader has to satisfy himself that all of the task force members understand the significance of their decision. It is a good idea to restate the problem once more. He should find at least one possible drawback, suggest one consequence that might be unfavorable. The point is that the solution needs a devil's advocate, and the objective of the chairman is to encourage the whole group to act in that role. If the solution cuts across departmental lines, the leader might suggest that each person in the task force evaluate the solution from the viewpoint of someone in his department who can be counted on to take a negative stand.

If the chairman gets a grudging response to his efforts to get the proper feedback, or if he senses that members are anxious to see the meeting over, he might consider proceeding no further until another meeting has been convened. The very superiority of a task force in decision-making is that the testing and feedback of a decision is simultaneous with the decision rather than delayed and too long after the fact, as it often is when the decision-making is sequential, bouncing from one involved department to another. It is this immediate testing and feedback that results in decisions that stick, that are right the first time. If he can't get this feedback, the chairman is well-advised to interrupt the process and resume it later when the members are refreshed and have recovered their perspective or developed critical data.

7. *Test the members' commitment.* This is the time to determine how involved and responsible the participants feel toward what has been decided. The chairman should satisfy himself that not only do his task force colleagues feel satisfied with the conclusion of their efforts but also with the way the goal was achieved. On occasion members of a group will agree with the solution that is reached but will harbor resentment—and hold back on commitment—because of the way it was reached (this might involve the behavior of other members, a suspicion of manipulation, etc.).

8. *Make sure of consensus.* The leader pushes for a firm statement that tells what the group has done and what it intends to do. He should be especially watchful for any signs of "going along" by any member. Ideally every participant is willing to subscribe publicly to what the task force has accomplished, and everyone is willing to see that accomplishment implemented. Above all, each member of the task force should manifest a proprietary interest in the solution and should feel that it is the best possible solution

under the circumstances. Otherwise, consensus may only be an illusion, and commitment to the decision may be inadequate.

SHARING THE LEADERSHIP

All of these formal roles should be performed by the leader. But they can be as effectively performed by any member of the group. And such performance should be encouraged and supported by the leader.

In closing this chapter, let me say unequivocally that the most important role of the leader is *to see that his leadership is shared by other members of the task force.* During the meetings there must be opportunities for other members to assume temporarily dominant roles. Usually this dominance is to enable a member to exercise his expertise in the area under consideration at that moment. But the assumption of leadership can be justified for other reasons—for example, a man's self-interest or the skills he possesses could enhance the group's deliberations at that point.

The point is that unless the leadership of the task force is available to be "borrowed" by other members, the chance is great that the resources of the group will be inadequately utilized.

One more reason why the formal leader must encourage others to take over the leadership role for periods of time is to offset his vested interests and subjectivity. If the chairman favors one idea or one member's contributions above others, then he can use his position to manipulate the meeting, to see that his own choice is presented in a better light than any other.

It serves the chairman's interest to encourage others to pre-empt his dominance and even to make sure they do it. If he doesn't, and if he takes undue advantage of his position, he risks having his leadership resented and challenged by those associates. Unfortunately, such a challenge usually interferes with the effectiveness of the group in reaching its assigned objectives.

NINE

EFFECTIVE BEHAVIOR
IN THE GROUP

Recently at a university-sponsored seminar for business-men, I joined in one of those inevitable discussions about the values of the younger generation. At one point, a personnel manager, a man in his late forties, contrasted his feelings about our country, its flag, and military service with those of the young people he knew. As he talked, his face became flushed, his voice rose in register and volume, and his gestures conveyed anger.

Later, over drinks, several participants reviewed the discussion; the personnel manager, noting the fact that some people during the session had shown anger, said, "I used to get upset about these things, but I don't any more."

After a few seconds of stunned silence, another man at

the table said, "Maybe you weren't upset, but you displayed all the symptoms."

The personnel manager looked surprised. "Really?"

The others around him nodded.

His reaction demonstrated a phenomenon often evident in small groups: A participant finds it difficult to assess his behavior and its impact on others. What we think we are doing is often quite different from what others see us doing.

That's one of the reasons for the rating forms used in the instrumented lab (see Chapter Six) so others can give us feedback on how they see our behavior, how they feel about what we are doing.

That we do not see ourselves as others in the group see us is one of four assumptions that can safely be made about most people in most group situations. Let's take a look at these assumptions and discuss them:

1. We need feedback from others to know how we are behaving.

2. A member of a group needs the support of other members to develop effective behavior.

3. To be effective in a group, we must learn to respect and express *feelings*.

4. Acceptance of the feelings of others is essential to understanding others.

AS OTHERS SEE US

> "Oh wad some power the giftie gie us
> to see oursels as others see us!"

So wrote poet Robert Burns some two hundred years ago. We may join in his lament. If we are not able on our own to see ourselves as others see us, then we have to rely on the others who *do* see us. We must develop knowledge of ourselves by using what others know of us.

But, of course, that's hardly easy. Most others do not look at us through unbiased eyes. There are qualities in us they admire or dislike, fear, envy, cannot identify with. Furthermore, they may like or dislike one quality so much that it puts all our other qualities in a shadow.

In a group, therefore, the reliability of my feedback to you depends chiefly on two factors: first, that you and I share a goal that makes it important for us to transcend our biases as much as possible, and second, that we trust each other.

Otherwise, my experience tells me I must be cautious, I must at least shave the truth. I don't want to give you feedback that might anger you or cause unpleasantness. And I don't want to risk hearing things about me from you that might hurt me or erode my self-esteem.

But when we have a goal that would be sufficiently important to achieve as to make the risks worthwhile, and when we can trust that each other is operating from a desire to attain that goal (and not from malice or selfishness), then we'll find it easier (although not necessarily painless) to exchange views of our behavior.

MUTUAL SUPPORT

Everyone in the group needs the support of everyone else to be effective. I want you to tell me when I am doing something that you feel helps the group.

"John, I don't know how the others feel, but I've noticed a few times that when our discussion strayed off the path, you stepped in and got us going again. And I think that's been a big help to us."

John will feel encouraged to step in again when he sees the discussion losing its way.

As a member, I also want you to tell me what I do that you feel gets in the way of effectiveness.

"Al, several times you've started your comments with, 'I'm upset about something I just heard.' But you seem so unruffled. I don't believe you're really that upset. So why don't you drop the phony opener and just come right out with what's on your mind? I'll accept what you say a lot better if I don't sit here and wonder if you really are upset."

Another irritating, ineffective behavior bites the dust.

But there are other supportive roles we can play. I can encourage you to introduce ideas: "That sounds interesting. Let's talk about it." You'd feel much better with that kind of reception than if I ignored your contribution or said, "That's a pretty silly idea."

I can make it easier for you to join in the discussion. "Some of us have dominated the discussion, and we haven't heard from Al in a long time. What do you think of this proposal, Al?"

If you are subjected to hostility, to attack, I can step in. "Phil, I don't think you're helping things by lashing out at Marv. You may have a gripe, but the way you put it turns me off. So, if I hear you right, what you are trying to tell Marv is . . ." I can help you to deal with the feedback better by stripping it of the hostility.

There are any number of roles I can play that support you in your efforts to help the group on its way to achieving whatever goal it has. And, of course, I need your support.

But it is no easy step for either of us to recognize and accept that individually we cannot be as effective as we want without the active help of other members of the group.

EXPRESSING FEELINGS

After an emotional session in a T group of which I was a member, one of the other participants, a young personnel researcher, said to me privately, "You know what you're asking of me? You want me to express my feelings, and I won't do it. Why, if I went back to my company and allowed myself to get emotional, I'd get cut right off at the pockets."

I didn't doubt him. The environment in many organizations proclaims, "Let's leave emotions out of this"; or, "Emotions have no place in this—let's be *reasonable.*"

Our puritanical heritage has much to do with this. We are taught to suppress expressions of feelings—to give vent to emotions is really not very nice, very dignified. Several times I have come across this definition of maturity: The ability to control emotions. That's the kind of maturity no one really needs. Our mental hospitals are full of people who achieved such "maturity."

We are rational *animals.* We have reason and passions. We learn on intellectual and emotional levels. We make rational and emotional commitments. Unfortunately, when the expression of feelings is not accepted, we intellectualize them. We dissect them as if they were lying on an operating table. Or we disguise them. The chances are that you can recall the frustration you felt when a particular colleague thoughtfully and with seeming objectivity opposed your ideas at every opportunity. You knew it was you he disliked—and he took out his animosity on your contributions. And he could smile when he did it!

Emotions have a place in our working lives. In fact, we cannot really be effective in our interactions with others if we ignore or disguise our feelings.

ACCEPTANCE IS NOT AGREEMENT

Often the reason why one man has trouble understanding others is that he has not learned to accept their feelings. Acceptance has no essential link with agreement, just as empathy does not necessarily lead to sympathy. When a man declares to me that he is petrified with fear because he is about to enter the hospital for minor surgery, I may be tempted to respond, "That's ridiculous. There's no cause for fear." Or when he charges me with wanting to "put him down" through a particular action of mine, I might indignantly say, "Nonsense. You have no right to feel that way."

In both cases I turn my back on his problem. He *feels* a certain way, and I tell him he has no right to feel that way, such feelings are uncalled for, and I may even imply that he does not in truth really feel that way at all.

Whether I believe he has a right to feel as he does, whether how he feels pleases me or not, whether in similar circumstances I would feel that way, these are not important considerations. Agreement and/or sympathy are not necessarily what he is asking for. He is asking me to *accept* his feelings. How easy it is for me to respond to him, "I can see that you are angry (or frightened). I know how you must feel."

By so doing I am not passing judgment on him. I am not giving his feelings legitimacy. I am simply acknowledging that he feels the way he says he feels.

A lot of people get stuck on this threshold of communications. One party becomes resentful over the other's refusal to understand or believe him, or the communication between them gets completely bogged down because the second man tries to prove to the first that he really feels what he says he is feeling.

And where emotions are concerned, it isn't possible to "prove" anything. And it isn't necessary anyway.

Thus, before you get into a discussion of his emotions, first accept what he says about them, even though you may suspect he is not correct in diagnosing his own feelings. The point is that he *feels* he feels this way, and there is no reason why others cannot accept that.

COURTESY AND COMMON SENSE

The evaluation forms that appear in Chapter Six indicate what specifically in the Organization Development Laboratory constitute helpful and effective behavior. And such behavior applies to nearly any group situation. While laboratory training is, as I've said, generally of value to most people who must work in small groups, developing effectiveness is to a large extent a matter of courtesy and common sense, awareness of your needs and the other man's.

Here are some chances for you to analyze some common group situations and to think through some tentative solutions. After reading the short problem, develop a recommended behavior on your own before you go on to my recommendation.

1. *You make a proposal to be considered by others in the conference.* At first, their reaction is polite attention, but noncommittal. After a time, however, one man begins to nod his agreement to some of your arguments. You decide to press on, feeling that his agreement is a good sign.

Recommendation: It can be a good sign, but there's a potential trap. The temptation is to continue to talk mainly to your new ally. But don't. You may undermine his power to help you by causing him to be labeled as your partisan. Also, by seeming to exclude others, you risk offending them.

2. *You present an idea, one that you feel strongly about.* Immediately, a colleague questions your idea in a way that makes you feel he is antagonistic toward it. His "attack" makes you angry, and you start to form your reply as an argument, in strong, hostile terms.

Recommendation: It's very human to want to defend yourself, and in this situation, you may feel that, if you don't leap to an immediate defense, his objection may spread to others. But before you do, make sure you really have all the information about his views.

Sometimes your silence will lead him to elaborate on his objection, and you may find that what you thought he said originally was not what he meant to say. Or someone else may try to answer for you. And this response will probably carry more weight than yours. Above all, don't interrupt someone who is challenging your views, even when you're sure he has missed your point. The fact that he is wrong doesn't rule out the possibility that he is telling you something you ought to hear.

3. *You are speaking to the group, but you sense no reaction from anyone around the table.* No one interrupts or shows signs of agreeing or disagreeing. You worry about making yourself clear, and you decide that since no one seems to be in a hurry to talk, you will continue until you get a reaction.

Recommendation: The problem with continuing to talk is that you have no assurance you will do any better at communicating than you have done so far. It's time to stop and ask, "Am I making myself clear?" Or, "I guess you have a question about this." Your purpose is to encourage someone to speak up and possibly give you a clue as to why you are not getting a response, and to indicate what direction you should take next.

4. *You make a suggestion which, before it is completely out, elicits a loud, despairing (and disparaging) groan from a colleague.* You stop speaking. Your first reaction is to respond to him aggressively, perhaps even to let him know that his ideas aren't so marvelous either, so how come . . .

Recommendation: Probably your other colleagues won't blame you for hitting back in the face of such rudeness. However, the lighter your response, the better. Chances are, his discourtesy has caused embarrassment around the table. You will be thanked silently by many if you relieve the tension. You have two good alternative actions: You can turn to the groaner and smile (dammit). "I gather," you say, "you don't go along with what I'm saying. Care to explain why?" Or you can draw in others in the group by saying something like: "One precinct heard from. Do others of you feel the same way? If so, I'll drop it." That is bound to spark some discussion, and your groaning colleague will probably be effectively defanged.

5. *You are telling a colleague why the idea he has just proposed is not workable.* He interrupts your reply with, "You've missed my point. That's not what I said." Patiently you explain why you know you did not miss his point, and repeat what he said.

Recommendation: When repeating what someone else has said, be careful not to let your pride get in your way. You may become so eager to prove that you are a good listener that you trap yourself in an argument over who said what. And others will not thank you for wasting their time.

Once again, two alternate tactics are preferable: Either say to the objector, "I may have missed your point. How does what you said differ from what I've been saying?" Or say to the others around the table, "I may be off. Did anyone else get the impression I did?" You may very well find that you are wrong. On the other hand, you may find yourself getting a lot of help.

GETTING ON WITH THE JOB

Here are other typical situations you often encounter in a meeting, with suggestions that will help you keep the meeting productive:

• If a colleague openly or even hostilely objects to what you are saying, listen to him carefully and look at him while he speaks. You are getting important feedback that tells you where you may not have performed effectively. If he becomes patently unfair, you may well find yourself defended by your colleagues—which is often much more effective than taking up the cudgel in your own behalf.

• Look for areas of agreement that you can call to the attention of the group. Even if these are minor matters, the group will develop a sense that it is getting on with the job. This will help you to move to a resolution of the larger issues.

• Make sure you get response from all the members of the group. From time to time, ask them whether they feel they've heard a clear presentation of a point. If all heads nod except one, say to him, "Do you have a reservation about this? Is there a question in your mind that should be answered?" In the case of a general lack of response, you'd be well advised to keep questioning frequently. Eventually someone will speak up and possibly give you a lead to what may be troubling several participants.

• If you feel hemmed in by challenges and objections, get help from others. For example, "I guess I haven't done justice to this," or "I guess I haven't made this clear. Can someone else here help me out?" The point is, place the blame for the lack of understanding (if that's what it is) on yourself. You may be surprised to find how much help you'll get in clarifying points or in closing gaps.

• Be realistic about the concessions you can afford to make. Sometimes your willingness to give up a minor point—"Of course, we can see that you get copies of the requisitions"—can make all the difference in getting acceptance of your major proposition. Know what you can afford—and cannot afford—to yield.

• Don't hesitate to ask for action on a proposal or a decision. This is one of the best ways to smoke out any hidden objectives or reservations that otherwise might not appear until after the meeting, if then.

TEAM-BUILDING ROLES

There is certain behavior that is generally recognized as essential to the success of any group session; such behavior requires no elaborate training. Chiefly what is required is the awareness (this is developable) that this behavior contributes substantially to attainment of task force objectives. Behavior of this kind is:

Encouraging. Until members of a group develop a high level of trust and respect for each other, they may be hesitant to speak freely. People can easily be intimidated and tend to censor themselves, especially if they feel others in the group are more knowledgeable or are, by virtue of office, in a position to form opinions of them that could be detrimental to their careers. It isn't easy to overcome these fears quickly. Especially in the early phase of the task force, people should not be submitted to harsh judgments as to the lack of value of their contributions. They should be invited frequently to speak up. When their contributions are good, they should be given recognition. It's not necessary or desirable to praise every contribution. Such recognition becomes meaningless, and people grow to resent the artificiality.

Harmonizing. Areas of disagreement seem so often to be emphasized more than points on which people agree. Each member of the group should discipline himself to talk first about where he agrees with others. And other members, as third parties, should also point out where two members agree. When this isn't done, people can waste a lot of time arguing with each other over apparent disagreement, when often there is no real discord.

Mediating. It's nearly impossible to make progress without conflict. I recall observing a T group in which everything was sweetness and light, and every member of the group was ready to boast about the harmony the group had achieved. The problem was that by implicit agreement they had avoided any issue that might have sparked controversy.

Accept conflict as natural. Don't be too hasty in stepping into a conflict. So long as two or more disputants are dealing with the issues, don't be concerned if there is some heat as well as light. But when they depart from the issues, or when they are no longer dealing effectively with their problems interacting with each other, then it is necessary to step in and redefine the issues they started to confront. If no one plays the mediator role, the disputants' attitudes will polarize—and so will those of some of the onlookers.

Gate-keeping. There are times when competition within the group is so keen that some members give up trying to battle the domination of others and keep quiet. Every member should be alert to the "withdrawal" of any other member and act to draw him back into the group. Usually, all that is necessary is to say, "We haven't heard anything from John on this. What do you think about it, John?"

Observing-Processing. Any group will benefit when, at one time or another, a member "steps back" and plays the role of observer—"processes" while the meeting goes on. Later, he can give members valuable feedback on what he saw happening, what others may have been too involved to notice, such as which behavior was effective, which was not, what was enhancing the progress of the group, what was hindering it, etc.

All of the above are informal leadership functions that anyone in a group can perform. As a leader, of course, you should be prepared to perform them *all the time*. And you'll want, by example and sometimes even by instruction, to encourage each member of your group to observe them in every meeting.

TEN

HOW TO HANDLE BEHAVIOR
YOU DON'T WANT

There are those who become uptight in any discussion about shaping behavior, especially the behavior of others. To them, the subject seems to smack of manipulation. But the truth is that all of us are being "shaped" all the time, often without knowing it. For example, I want to persuade a colleague to take on a certain assignment. If he reacts enthusiastically to my description, if he assents to my request, I know my behavior has been effective. I have attained my goal. His feedback and my success both help to encourage me to use the same kind of persuasion the next time I want him to do me a favor.

Sometimes we see examples of behavior that seem to us to be so ineffective as to be self-defeating. And we may ask, "How can he do that?" Or, "Can't she see that she offends everyone when she acts that way?"

In some cases the answer is that he and she have felt they were effective with such behavior. In other contexts, they were reinforced either by feedback from others, or achievement of goals, or both. But what they forget is that goals change. What these people with obstructive behavior don't realize is that in *your* group success is measured in very different terms from that of other groups with which they have been associated.

For example, let's take a look at a favorite organizational sport: putting down the ideas of others. Some people are very expert at this, as you'll see in the four profiles following. They have had considerable practice, and their successful idea-killing has reinforced such group behavior. And these people may even have been applauded by their associates; they have enjoyed a reputation for their negativism.

Here are four common members of the species:

• *The sandwich-maker.* The top slice of bread is thin praise. "I must say that Bob has certainly spent a lot of time and done a lot of thinking on this. It shows." But the meat of the sandwich is fat with scorn. Point by point, the sandwich-maker shows that, while there may have been a lot of thinking, all told it doesn't add up to very much quality. The bottom slice of bread is also praise: "I'm sorry to have spent so much of the group's time making my comments, but I felt that Bob's tremendous effort deserves the most detailed treatment."

• *The guru.* Patience is his idea-killing method. While the idea is discussed by others, he sits, contemplatively gazing at the wall or at the table. His face wears a melancholy expression. He will not speak until he is called upon, which is usually well into the discussion. Because of his long and thoughtful silence, and because the meeting chairman has invited him to participate, his contribution carries added weight. And his negativism somehow seems to be an eminently reasonable position.

• *The nibbler.* His weapon against ideas is trivia. He talks quite a bit during the meeting, but he never goes after the substantial matters. He wears the group down by nibbling away at the edges. Everyone else on the task force is concerned with staffing the new product group. He, however, is fixated on the question of who on the staff will have drapes and carpets. He is so persistent and annoying that a proposed new procedure may sometimes be dropped in favor of retaining the old, simply because his nibbling makes the change appear to be so much more involved than it is.

• *The pathologist.* He kills ideas by intimidation. Like the guru, he generally remains silent during the meeting. But after the conference, he does a thorough job of dissecting in a series of post-mortems. He goes from office to office, asking, "Did you see what was really going on in there?" His ingenuity and imagination provide an entertaining, sometimes devastating, interpretation of the actions, motivations, and schemes of his colleagues in the meeting. One reason why he doesn't speak up more is that he wants to remain unsullied as an observer.

The damage a pathologist does is not confined to these post-mortems. Fear of his dissecting talents can intimidate his colleagues at future meetings and thereby inhibit effective group consideration of ideas.

Obviously you don't want such kinds of activity on your task force. You want to discourage this damaging behavior while developing the person himself as a resource (or at the very least you want to neutralize his bad effects on the other members of the group).

The first step is to tell the idea-killer privately that his negative behavior subverts the creative efforts of others. He may not have realized what he was doing, and learning about it may lead him to alter his behavior. It's more likely, however, that the behavior is so ingrained he cannot change it without help. Here, then, is what you can do:

• *Trim the sandwich-maker.* He hides behind a façade of even-handedness, of giving both praise and criticism. But the praise is only window dressing. If you are chairman, make him spell out first what he considers good, and *only* what he likes. Tell him to reserve criticism until later. Then get positive comments from others. Later, come back to him and repeat the process to get the negative side. Don't let him mix the pluses and minuses. Chances are that, using this approach, you'll cut back his negative impact, for several reasons:

1. Without the façade of praise, his criticism will be more stark than ever before. He'll probably soften it.
2. He will probably try to beef up his positive comments when they must stand on their own.
3. By alternating his comments with those of others, you lessen his speechmaking opportunity.

• *Goad the guru.* One way to keep him from killing ideas is to ignore him. If he doesn't ask to speak, don't ask him. A more positive technique is to say, toward the end of a meeting in which he has not spoken, "Does anyone else want to comment?" Don't use his name or look very long in his direction. If he wants to join in, he'll have to make the first move—and that will blunt his effect.

Both of these techniques, however, may serve to keep him quiet. And if you feel he has something to contribute, then a third approach may be more constructive: Call on him by name, but do it early in the discussion before he has built the mystical aura. Also, by getting him into the act early, you'll have a better chance to balance his negativism either through your own remarks or through others' comments.

• *Force-feed the nibbler.* It's no use trying to head off this man's negative feelings toward ideas by suggesting that what he wants to talk about are not important matters, because he'll respond by saying, "I think they are important." That has all the makings of an impasse, unless you break it by giving in. *He* won't yield. Rather, you must keep guiding him to the substantial issues, keep trying to get him to tell you how he feels about the really important aspects. This is not his area of strength, and you'll be better able to exercise some control over him. You won't be entirely successful in keeping him off trivia, but you will lessen the impact of his nibbling by forcing him to take some bigger bites now and then.

• *Pin down the pathologist.* The antidote to this man's idea-killing tendencies is to get him to contribute more in the meetings themselves. The point is that by participating he loses his status as observer. Say to him, "Joe, I know you're going to have some questions on this after the meeting. Let's see whether we can answer them now."

THE POWER OF NEGATIVE THINKING

However a manager chooses to handle negative or obstructive behavior, one thing is certain: He should *not* ignore it. The hard truth is that such behavior can have a crippling effect on group effort, especially in its early stages. The chances are that nearly any manager can recall meetings in which progress was brought to a halt by someone's suggestion that the group table the proposal, hold off on a decision for one reason or another, or simply kill the idea.

It's discouraging but true that a negative vote seems to carry so much weight when there is a certain risk involved in voting "aye," because in the face of uncertainty, it is perfectly understandable to hold off making a decision, to take that extra look. And it's just as human to want to be able to ally oneself with the I-told-you-so side when the venture proves to be unworkable. It's a *safety reaction* in the face of risk.

Understanding why people respond so quickly to a negative voice is small comfort to the manager who wants a positive action taken on a project that is close to him. And, of course, there is the possibility that a negative or delaying vote is justified.

But people seem not to demand the same justification for a "nay" that they do for an "aye." And, as a member of a task force, you will want to make sure the "nay" can be justified.

You may not, in a decision-making situation, have a strong, personal stake in the particular matter to be resolved. Nevertheless, you'll want to be on the alert for the counterproductive, negative, roadblocking action that can so easily nullify the progress of a group that is working toward a solution. It isn't, of course, that nay-saying is automatically bad; but it is true that nay-saying is easier than taking a risk, and should be just as critically looked at as partisanship in the other direction. Here are counteractions you can take:

• *Explain what is at stake.* In a decision in which there is risk, no one wants to be tagged with having made a mistake. But there are times when that tag is less deadly than at other times. In some cases, if the decision proves to be a mistake, it will hardly bankrupt you. Or if the decision is not made, there will be searching questions from higher management as to why no action was taken. So put the decision in perspective. Show that the stakes are not as high as people seem to think, and that the consequences of not making a positive decision could be a greater evil to all concerned than taking a step that falls short of success.

• *Handle a challenge to your leadership.* Sometimes in pushing for a project you can anticipate that opposition will come not because of the other man's disagreement with your ideas but from his opposition to your "leadership" in presenting the idea. Generally you can recognize this opposition for what it is. It probably isn't the first time he has shown such behavior.

When you find yourself faced with such a challenge to your leadership, work to get the discussion out of the arena you find yourself in. For example, you might say,

"I guess everyone can see how Sam and I feel. So I suggest we hear more from the people who haven't said much."

If *you* can't be the leader, then multiply the leadership.

° *Sell the advantages.* In those decision-making situations in which a negative vote receives what you consider to be undue attention, you may discover that the advantages of making a positive decision outweigh the disadvantages. "Okay," you might point out, "perhaps this may fail, and some people will be a little unhappy because we decided to risk it. But we'll get some data we couldn't obtain any other way."

You may, in fact, have more tangible benefits to offer from a go-ahead decision. But the point is that whatever good things could come out of a risky decision should be re-emphasized in case some members of the group didn't recognize the pulses the first time around.

° *Confront the behavior.* The man who is throwing up opposition to a positive decision—or, indeed, to any decision—may not be entirely aware of the obstructive role he is playing (although he may be sensitive to the possibility that others may feel he is playing an obstructive role). In some situations, you may want to pin him down: Why does he want to hold off? Or why does he think the dangers outweigh the benefits? What's the worst that can happen if a positive decision is made? (Learn to ask the question, "Why not?")

It might be sufficient to say to him, "Look, I think you are closing out the chances to consider this fairly." He may not agree, but you may get vital support from others.

MUZZLING THE MONOPOLIZER

Ironically, some of the most obstructive behavior comes from the man who desperately wants to contribute, who wants his colleagues to look upon him as a valuable member of the team. But he more often is considered a pest—he monopolizes the group sessions.

He talks—and talks—and talks. It isn't that he has nothing to say. More often, it's just that he takes so long to get it said, and in the process he prevents others from making their contributions. Ironically, outside the meeting, his behavior may be quite different: considerate, constructive, cooperative. But put him in a group situation, and he becomes pushy, hoggish, hard to control. (If his behavior is more constructive outside the group, that is a good sign that he is not trying to compete with you for leadership. This can be an altogether different problem than the poor meeting manners we are discussing here.)

There may be any number of reasons why an individual tries to dominate the meeting. He is seeking the esteem of his colleagues (and usually failing to get it). He is an exhibitionist. He has an image problem (one manager I know thinks of himself as a creative person—and apparently he is convinced that creative people are never silent). He is an old pro: "Back in 1951 we . . ."

But what is more important than understanding the motives of the monopolizer is finding ways to influence his behavior, to get him to moderate his activities in a conference room.

To begin with, there are four "don'ts" that the leader should observe:

• *Don't manipulate.* Here's one example of manipulation: Place the "pest" at your side (or even slightly to your rear) so that you can seemingly overlook his efforts to get your attention. Another is to acknowledge his bid for attention, ask him to defer his comments till later, then call on him a minute or two before adjournment. But I suggest that there's really no excuse to rig the meeting against him when there are honest techniques available.

• *Don't humiliate.* Using sarcasm, "Now listen to the expert"; making audible groans when he starts speaking; discriminating against him by setting rules that apply to him only: "All right, you've got exactly five minutes and no more."

• *Don't abdicate.* When you let him talk as much as he wants, when you decline to interfere with his rambling or to control the time he spends, then you surrender control of the meeting to the monopolizer. When a chairman abdicates his control in favor of the excessive talker, he is plainly unfair to the others in the group.

• *Don't reinforce.* This is the most subtle admonition of all. When you protect him, or keep others from shutting him off, you risk encouraging his offensive behavior. Paradoxically, if you argue with him, you may also be reinforcing the behavior you don't want. Here are two cases where this may happen:

1. He insists on arguing every trivial point, even semantics (especially when he has no substantial evidence to back up his argument).

2. He does not hesitate to take the argument out of the mainstream and off at a tangent.

In either of these cases, arguing with him may be reinforcing him and defeating yourself.

There are steps you can take, singly or in collaboration with other members, that will help you control the conference hog but will at the same time help you to enjoy the contributions he can make:

1. *Tell him what a pest he is.* Talk with him privately about his talkiness. But this will work only if he is conscious of his behavior or has enough trust in you to accept your description of what he does.

However, this kind of trust level is usually not found in the formative stages of a group, and this kind of maturity (or at least awareness of one's own behavior) is not found in most individuals. Where these are lacking, all that your talking to the offender will accomplish is to raise his defenses and shut him off altogether.

2. *One point at a time.* When he has made a point, and is rambling on to another, interrupt him to reinforce the one point he has made so far and suggest that it ought to be discussed. Then ask others for their reactions to the point he has made.

3. *Go around the table.* Let him understand that while he has the privilege of speaking, everyone else shares that privilege. Once he has made a point, explain to him that you want to go around the table to insure that everyone else gets an equal chance.

4. *Make him clarify.* Once he has begun to ramble or become disorganized, stop him and tell him that you are not certain you understand what he has been saying. Put pressure on him to clarify. In that way, you'll force him to think through more carefully the point he has made, and you'll make it more difficult for him to go on to a second point immediately.

5. *Concede minor points.* Too often, minor or inessen-

tial points become the foci of arguments. And very often, the monopolizer can be "controlled" if others concede minor points that appear to be very major to him. For example, "Okay, on the first report of the month, we extend the deadline from Tuesday to Wednesday."

6. *Make him write down his ideas before.* Suggest to him the scope of the meeting before it is called, and ask him either to write down what he considers the main points or to make an outline. Don't hesitate to tell him why you are asking this: You want to help him be more effective in the conference. Then during the meeting ask him to refer to his outline as he talks.

The important thing to keep in mind is that, with the compulsive talker, the rambler, the monopolizer, no one-time action is going to be effective. You are aiming for a change of behavior, and this takes time. The behavior you want must be defined and reinforced by techniques such as those above. What makes these legitimate techniques rather than manipulations is the honesty of the chairman as to his objectives in using them: to increase the effectiveness of the monopolizer and to decrease the inhibiting effect he may have on the success of the meeting.

THE SILENT ONE

At the other end of the spectrum is the man who sits at meetings week after week and never opens his mouth. He is one of your vital resources. He probably knows his area of the business very well. Probably, too, he communicates well on a one-to-one basis. But put him in a group situation and the tape goes over his mouth. Not only do you lose an important human asset, his silence may throw the whole group off its stride if others decide he is not pulling his load.

Here are some techniques to help the "clam" participate in a conference:

• Call on him for his experience or specialty. "This is something that Jim has had a lot of experience with; let's hear from him on it."

• Tell him in advance that a certain topic is going to come up. Ask him to prepare a comment. Then at the appropriate moment in the meeting feed him a cue line.

• Feed him questions he can handle: "How does the breakdown procedure on this equipment look to you?" or "Did you ever run into this kind of situation when you were out in the field?"

• Give him time to compose what he is going to say. Try calling on one or two others in the group before calling on the clam. That way you can tip him off and give him time to prepare an answer.

THE HIDDEN AGENDA

One of the most serious obstacles to the effectiveness of a group session is what behavioral scientists refer to as the *hidden agenda,* which results from prejudices, personality conflicts, or leadership aspirations that members bring into the conference room. For example, A has introduced a proposal, a suggestion of a certain action to be conducted before the next meeting. The proposal meets with favor, and it seems logical to ask A to assume the responsibility for taking action (to make a study, to take a trip, to form a subgroup, or whatever). Member B secretly approves of the action, but he disapproves of the delegation to A. Instead of simply stating his objection, B systematically tries to block progress on the proposal. His agenda, known only to B, is to prevent A from playing a productive role.

Some agendas are more involved and even harder to detect. If you are chairman, you may find another member challenging your leadership by making you look ineffective or by promoting himself.

Once again, let me caution that you cannot afford to ignore the unstated agenda.

There are several steps a leader can take to help the group and its members work out hidden agendas so that real progress toward the stated objectives can be made:

• *Look for the hidden agendas.* Don't try to pretend they don't exist. You won't get rid of their effect by rigidly insisting that the group stick to the stated subject.

• *Bring them up.* One way to bring hidden agendas to the surface is to say something like this: "I wonder whether we've said all we feel about this matter? Why don't we take some more time to see if there are any more thoughts?"

• *But don't force them up.* Some agendas are better left "under the table." Sometimes they can be worked out better by the people involved without bringing the rest of the group into it.

• *Don't make them embarrassing.* Don't embarrass any members of the group by chiding them about their hidden agendas. In one meeting I attended, a manager listened for a time to a cautious interchange between his colleagues, then announced boldy, "All I can hear is someone grinding an ax." Not only did progress stop on working out the hidden agendas, but those who had been talking fell silent on the stated agenda as well.

People have a natural way of working out what's on their minds, although much that goes on in meetings can seem diversionary. To scold or try to shame them into an adherence to prestated guidelines can itself be disruptive.

You can't, of course, have any insurance that bringing up hidden agendas won't disrupt the purported business of the meeting. But if you consider that the real purpose of the meeting is to meet objectives rather than mere agendas, you'll have a much better chance of ultimately fulfilling such objectives.

HANDLING CONFLICTS

Every task force leader must confront the possibility of a feud between two or more members of the group. Should he intervene? In most cases, probably not, unless their behavior toward one another is adversely affecting their performance, and possibly even the effectiveness of others (through such behavior as introducing hidden agendas into meetings). If that is the case, there are at least two options open to you:

1. Personally step into the conflict and let them know what damage their behavior is doing. But avoid the temptation to try to influence their feelings toward each other. No matter how much you'd like them to feel more friendly toward each other, you probably won't succeed in changing their attitudes. You may even have to suggest that, if they cannot stop the disruptive behavior, one will be asked to resign from the task force.

2. Let the group act as a third party. With the consent of the other members, encourage the disputants to discuss any work-related problems between them before the whole group. And with the consent of the feuding members, ask the other members of the group to comment freely on the issues as they see them. Perhaps the conflict can't be entirely resolved, but with the help of the group, the disputants can work through some of the problems and alleviate some of the points in conflict.

But even if you don't intervene, you will want to make sure you don't inadvertently exacerbate the conflict. Here are some guidelines to follow:

• *Don't take sides.* When the complaints you hear from people in conflict are general ones, you may feel tempted to simply agree with whoever happens to be speaking at the moment—to nod, or otherwise indicate that you are "with him." This is particularly true if you like the man, or find even a grain of truth in the complaint he is voicing about the other.

There can also be the temptation to disagree, if personally you and he are not close or if you feel he is being unfair to his colleague.

But it is best to let them work it out themselves, without your implied support of one or the other to use as a weapon. If you have the trust of both men, joining the feud could jeopardize your own effectiveness with them.

• *Judge the issue, not the people.* There are times, of course, when you may have to make a judgment about a task force-related matter about which the members disagree. And you know that, if you decide one way, you will seem to be boosting one subordinate; if you decide the other way, your action will be interpreted as supporting his opponent. But try to keep personalities out of the decision. Judge the merits of the arguments alone. Try not to let the possible political repercussions of your respective choices influence your action.

In announcing your decision, try as much as possible to make both men aware of the real, work-related reasons why you made your choice. This minimizes your own addition to their war.

• *Don't extend favors to one or the other.* The minute you start extending any sort of favors to one over the other, you are, perhaps unwittingly, taking sides in the conflict. Such favors can extend from seemingly innocent pieces of information—advance notices, in-depth backgrounds, supplementary data—to such actual assistance as access to additional secretarial help or to the bending of rules and procedures for special situations.

• *Don't speak for one to the other.* This is another way a manager can unwittingly get caught in the middle between two antagonistic colleagues. One may be talking to you about something the other did or said, and you feel the critic is being unfair. So you try to justify or explain the other man's actions or words. In the process you can't help but inject your own understanding of what one man meant, which may be offensive to the critic. And so you are just complicating the misunderstanding further.

A better course might be to indicate to the man who is complaining to you that he really ought to take up the matter directly with the other man—to let the other man speak and clarify his actions for himself.

TAKEOVER BY AN OUTSIDER

Occasionally another member of management may sit on a meeting of your task force. Even though he is a guest, he may yield to the temptation to dominate the session. If he is a person of considerable authority, that domination will be hard to deal with.

The boss who dominates a meeting chaired by his subordinate is a problem to himself and to his subordinate. He can cause others at the meeting to resent his monopolizing things. Your image is eroded among your peers if you take a back seat to the guest. Even if there isn't resentment, there very often is a feeling among other participants of intimidation: "Who is going to go against the big man?" So participation falls off. The meeting gets sidetracked; it doesn't go where you wanted it to go.

Let's start with the assumption that in a lot of cases when an executive is invited to a meeting, he's not sure what role he's expected to play. So here are some steps you can take to let him—and others in the meeting—know what his function and status are in your conference:

• *Tell him.* "John, I know there are areas of the company's financial picture that you know better than we, and I'd like you to help us out in those areas." He now has a rough idea of what you expect him to do in your meeting.

When you introduce him to the group or acknowledge his presence, stress the fact that you have *invited* him, and give your reason for it. "John indicates he is willing to answer questions we might have about the big financial picture." Such an explanation conveys to everyone the message that the guest is not there to wade into the discussion but is rather a resource to be utilized by the group.

If his presence is needed for only part of the meeting, let him know how long you estimate he'll be there. "You can expect to be out of the conference by two o'clock at the latest."

• *Take charge from the outset.* Some managers get their colleagues' attention, then ask the visitor to make opening remarks. But you'll avoid problems and misunderstanding if you make the opening remarks or define the problem yourself. Then call on him only at the point where his special knowledge will be helpful.

When you want to signal that you'd like to move on to another subject in which his participation isn't needed, say something such as, "I'd like to thank John for taking time out of his schedule to meet with us. We're going to move on to the XY-8 project now. John, if you'd like to sit in on that, you're welcome. Or if you would rather leave, we understand." In that way you can define for him his role as a listener rather than as a participant.

Your behavior—what you say, what you do—should provide everyone with a clue to what you expect of him. If it is a minimum role you want of him, then the less you single him out on any idea or comment, the better.

What you have to bear in mind constantly is that his rank does influence your behavior—and, of course, the behavior of your colleagues—toward him. Whatever his rank and influence, he deserves the courtesy of as much explanation and role definition as you can give him before the meeting. If you've neglected the preliminaries, and if he seems to take over, then you'll find it more difficult, and undoubtedly embarrassing to everyone in the room, to let him know what channels you expect him to confine himself to.

If for any reason the guest does in fact monopolize your meeting, don't engage him in a public debate on who's running the meeting. You'll only create an unproductively tense climate around the table. Your best step is to see him privately after adjournment and tell him how you feel about his domination. He probably was not aware of his behavior, and once he realizes what he has done, he'll be more likely to work with you to make sure he doesn't repeat his gaffe.

After all, his image of himself is undoubtedly just as important to him as yours is to you.

SOME COMMON BARRIERS

Most of the behavior we have discussed thus far in this chapter is occasional, or limited to the disruptive activities of a few people. Let's turn now to behavior that nearly everyone in a group session falls into, behavior that can inhibit the group's effectiveness.

Shutting off. B responds to something that A has just said: "That's the most ridiculous thing I've ever heard." Or "Your facts are all wrong." These are merely two of the almost infinite number of ways to shut off another member of the group, to prevent him from being effective. In fact, one technique for shutting him off is to keep him from making his point at all by interrupting with a remark that may or may not be related to what he has been saying. Of course, there are more subtle ways to gag him—humor, for example: Take some aspect of his point and turn it into a joke. By the time everyone gets through laughing, what he was saying has lost its impact.

You should recognize that, even if the shutting off is unintentional, the man interrupted often will not only drop his efforts to make his point, but will even abstain from further activity within the group. He withdraws without leaving the room.

As soon as possible, ask the man who has been a shut-off victim a question like this: "Did you get a chance to finish? Was there anything you wanted to add?" You may even wish to let him know you think he was shut off by saying, for example, "I have a feeling we didn't give A a chance to finish his point, and I'd like to hear him out."

Judging behavior. B says to A, "There's no reason for you to get mad about it." This is what is called being *judgmental* or *evaluative* about another's behavior. And sometimes it seems reasonable. A's face was red, his voice came in spurts and became much louder than usual. But his first impulse may be to deny he was angry (and in fact he may not have realized that he was). What happens then is that he drops the issue he was discussing to argue that he was not at all angry.

Putting a label on another man's behavior, such as "You're defensive," or "You're not being honest," often results in sidetracking the group's business while the labeled one tries to purge himself of the charge.

If you are giving feedback to the other fellow on his feelings, restrict your observations to how his feelings affect you or how you *think* he feels. He can't dispute how you feel. He doesn't have to defend himself. He can simply not agree with your perception. If others dispute the feelings or feedback, then the leader might step in to ask A whether in truth he was angry. If he says, "No," everyone (including B) should accept it and press on to other issues.

Analyzing. "You're projecting," or "You sound as if you're being threatened." It seems as if everyone today is tempted to play amateur analyst, to tell his colleagues not only what they are doing but why they are doing it. One man's diagnosis of another may be true, but he can't really know for sure. It's a trap—and a good one to avoid.

You must be especially on guard for this sidetracking technique. Sometimes it is necessary to be quite blunt to forestall it: "Let's listen to what A has to say. I think we're really more interested in what he is saying than in guessing why he is saying it. In fact, suppose we let him tell us why he is saying it, *if he wants to.*"

Not listening. Actually, much of the misunderstanding that is evident in any meeting is a result of poor listening. The fact is that many people do not listen well. One reason why is that our personal biases get in the way of our analyzing objectively what is being said. That's why so much time is spent by people rebutting things that were never really said.

If as leader you encounter much of this during your conference, suggest that, to save time and increase understanding, each person, before commenting on another's point, repeat the latter's point in essence and get his agreement that that is actually what he meant. Then, at least, the rebuttal or analysis has a better chance of being on target.

Blocking. There are innumerable ways a participant can

prevent another member or the entire group from getting on with its business. Humor is one. I am sure we have all seen the damage that can be done by a "clown" who interrupts serious, constructive effort with humorous sallies that prevent things from being said that should be said. I remember a meeting in which the real business of the group was stalled while two members engaged in a private agenda. A third member tried to get the meeting back on the track, but his efforts were stymied by a fourth man who made a joke at the third man's expense, a joke that implied that he did not understand what was really going on. Most people in the group sympathized with the third man's efforts to get the meeting going again, but the laughter and ridicule destroyed his ability to influence the group. The private argument continued to the frustration of nearly everyone.

Another blocking tactic succeeds when a member takes the spotlight to talk of a side issue or to talk about something that occurred outside the group.

As chairman, your response to blocking is to suggest that the main threads be picked up where they were dropped before the blocking. And if one man in the group has been largely responsible for the blocking, you may have to call attention to what he has been doing.

Blocking often occurs when the group is confronting an uncomfortable issue, and any attempt to get the deliberation sidetracked to "safe" issues is often welcomed. It is a very human response to unpleasantness or risk, but a serious group will usually respond positively to the suggestion that they have retreated from confrontation.

Laboratory training, as we have indicated, is useful for learning to recognize different kinds of behavior that can be obstructive and for dealing with them. In this chapter we have covered behavior that is easily recognized and, for the most part, can be dealt with by any member of the group. While the recommendations have been to a great extent addressed to the formal leader of the group, calling attention to and getting around obstructive behavior is, of course, the job of every member of a task force. And one of the most important functions of the team leader is to equip, help, and encourage his colleagues to play such corrective roles—through calling attention to the obstructive behavior, through his example in avoiding it, and through his support of any member who undertakes action against undesirable and unhelpful behavior on the part of others.

ELEVEN

EVALUATION AND FOLLOW-UP

A frequent mistake made by task force leaders is their failure to consistently evaluate the effectiveness of their group sessions and to insure a follow-up of the action decided upon by the task force. Evaluation and follow-up techniques serve several vital purposes:

• They keep the problem or issue and the objective before the members. As I have pointed out, during the life of a task force, problems change in definition (with a corresponding change in objectives), old constraints are removed and new ones imposed, and new resources are discovered. So it is necessary to keep everyone on the track, especially between meetings.

• Such techniques are needed to make meetings more effective. There must be a sufficient opportunity for everyone to contribute, for all of the resources to be tapped. The climate of the session should encourage openness and leveling. The leadership (formal and informal) must insure that issues are squarely confronted.

• They help you build an effective team, both in and outside of meetings. The task force must coalesce as a group, a point at which all members think primarily in terms of what helps the group meet its objectives. This is not to say that personal goals are discarded, only those personal goals or behaviors that impede the group's progress.

One sign that a group has actually formed is the substantial reduction in (and perhaps even disappearance of) those post-mortems that people conduct with those others in the group with whom they feel most comfortable and in which they say in private what should have been said in the meeting.

• They help you measure the progress of the group and its members. It is important to operate with a timetable, and you can't be sure of a realistic schedule without a method of measurement. Too, the organization is employing the task force to develop personnel resources, and there must be an effective way to judge the growth and progress of task force members.

• Evaluation and follow-up techniques help prevent the slippage that often occurs between a decision and its implementation. Decisions often come to grief because people get tired of arguing and seem to agree, when they really don't. There is, at best, resignation—there is not commitment. Also, a person often leaves a group session remembering what he wants to remember, which in some cases may be inadequate for carrying out the group's wishes. Finally, second thoughts color a man's picture of the meeting. Each member of the task force needs objective follow-up.

• They help top management build data on task force effectiveness. What problems are best handled by teams? What is a realistic schedule? What is the optimum mix of people and specialties?

MEETING EFFECTIVENESS

The forms illustrated in Chapter Six, those used in the Organization Development Laboratory, can serve as indicators of both group and individual effectiveness. The forms should be completed after each meeting. The task force leader might schedule a brief post-meeting session immediately following the group deliberation so that the evaluations made by each member can be recorded. It is preferable that each person's evaluation be given publicly, so that other members can ask him for the basis of his evaluations.

Subsequently, the task force leader can distribute the over-all, average ratings derived from the individual evaluations. In addition, he might provide space for the following:

• A reprise of the actions taken or recommendations made during the meeting recently concluded.
• A clear statement of what is to be done (and by whom) before the next session.

• Any thoughts or contributions a member developed after adjournment.

• The question: What specifically does each task force member believe could be done to improve the effectiveness of the next meeting?

One experienced task force leader, while he does not ask his associates to evaluate each session, periodically schedules two- or three-day simulation sessions to stimulate the processing. Such a periodic team-building session is undoubtedly beneficial, but a lot of interaction problems can develop between such sessions and cause a great deal of damage until they are recognized and worked out in the periodic labs.

However, confronting personnel problems as they arise is not the only value to an evaluation program during the life of a task force. Or perhaps even greater value is that when task force participants act in an effective manner, their success should be acknowledged and reinforced through high ratings. There can be as much learning accomplished through success as through failure.

To supplement members' own evaluations of their and the group's efforts, there is the technique of "fishbowling." A selected group of executives or another task force are invited to observe a meeting of the group. The session is conducted as any other. The observers do not participate. However, after the meeting, the onlookers are encouraged to give feedback to the task force on what they observed, especially as to the process. Of course, those who are observing must be acquainted with processing, and those who are observed must accept the visitors' comments *without challenge*. The task force may discuss the feedback after their visitors have left. The important thing is that no visitor should be submitted to "punishment" because of comments that may be unfavorable to task force members.

LEVELING

Periodically, every few sessions, task force members could be asked to provide personal feedback for one another such as is provided for in the forms illustrated in Chapter Six. Several things are accomplished by the use of such forms. First, the leveling is controlled; it is restricted to the behavior categorized on the form, thus reducing the chance that people will give feedback that reflects prejudice or that is irrelevant to the group concerns. Second, the forms train the participants to eventually deliver the same kind of feedback, to "process," as the behavior occurs in the meeting itself. Third, task force members are preparing for peer evaluation that is recommended at the conclusion of the project.

When the task force has completed its work and has been phased out, a summary rating of the group's effectiveness should be prepared to elicit the following information:

1. The effectiveness of the group leadership.

2. The suitability of this kind of problem for task force effort.

3. The effectiveness of membership selection criteria, whether the time schedule for achievement of the group's objective was realistic, and what follow-up is desirable (for example, should certain members of the task force be asked to monitor the activity that has grown out of the group's work, or should another task force be selected to

explore a tangential issue that arose during the primary problem-solving effort, etc.).

The periodic evaluations and the final summary should provide management with data to guide them in future task force assignments and organization.

WOULD YOU WORK WITH HIM AGAIN?

Evaluation of each member of the task force by his colleagues is equally important. Ideally, task force members should evaluate each other—openly. Peer evaluation is as yet an avant-garde concept in our corporations. Few question its value or logic. It is felt, however, that most people are not quite ready emotionally to be judged by those with whom they work, those who have no authority over them.

But a team should break through his emotional barrier. Once again, the forms in Chapter Six can be adapted. The following data, at least, should be elicited for each task force member (ratings on a scale of 1 to 10 or percentages of 1 to 100):

• The value of his contributions.
• The over-all effectiveness of his performance in the group in helping the team reach its goals.
• How effective is he in initiating ideas, supporting others in introduction of their ideas, and working to establish a collaborative climate?
• How open is he? Does he consistently level?
• To what extent is he goal- or results-oriented?

Additionally, these questions might be asked:

• Would he, in your opinion, be suitable to lead a task force?

• Would you be willing to work with this man on another task force if the problem fell within his area of competence?

Ideally, task force members should openly exchange their evaluation of each other. But if this degree of leveling is thought too risky, then the members can submit their evaluation privately to the task force leader, who, in addition to supplying his own appraisal of each member, answers the following question provided on the forms submitted by members in their peer evaluation: "Do you substantially agree or disagree with this evaluation?" If he disagrees, he should provide an explanation.

All rating forms are then submitted to the executive overseer of the task force and/or to the respective permanent manager to be used in the regular appraisal program.

The task force leader should, if possible, discuss the written evaluations with each member's regular manager. The latter has responsibility for his subordinate's compensation, future assignments, and promotions, and the manager needs to reconcile the data from the task force with his own criteria for advancement of the subordinate. Although the task force manager may not have the authority to provide advancement for the man he has been working with during the period, he may very well, in his discussions with the regular manager, wish to make recommendations relating to compensation, type of work assignments, transfer, etc.

Since I have gone so far in advocating openness and a multiplicity of evaluations, let me go one step farther to urge that the task force member's regular manager discuss these evaluations with him, if not at the phasing out of the team then certainly during the next appraisal period.

I am hardly unaware that in endorsing peer group evaluation, I shall cause some managers no little discomfort. But the idea of charging *one* man alone with the evaluation of another is absurd. We are all biased. We all have limited perceptions of others. We are all capable of responding defensively to threats to us posed by the attitudes and skills of others.

Nothing, it seems to me, makes better sense, or is fairer, than to have a man evaluated by as many people in as many different situations as possible and as often as any significant appraisal of him can be made.

TWELVE

THE NEW SOCIETY

"I home to America," wrote British author Anthony Burgess recently in *The New York Times,* "as to a country more stimulating than depressing. The future of mankind is being worked out there . . ."

Probably many Americans find it hard to share his optimism in the face of the widespread discontent and dissent in this country. But it is this very dissent that leads another foreign observer, the Frenchman Jean-François Revel, to agree in essence with Burgess. In his provocative book, *Without Marx or Jesus,* Revel declares, "The revolution of the twentieth century will take place in the United States. It is only there that it can happen. And it has already begun."

It is in the context of this revolution—and I agree that it is precisely that—that this book should be read. I have, it is true, devoted most of this book to a specific technique, task force management. But the underlying assumption throughout is that we are on the threshold of a profound cultural change. The task force is at once a symbol of, and a means to further, this change.

Revel provides a clue to the nature of this change. "There is," he writes, "a basis common to all manifestations of the American revolt, and to its European extension. That basis consists in the rejection of a society motivated by profit, dominated exclusively by economic considerations, ruled by the spirit of competition, and subjected to the mutual aggressiveness of its members. Indeed, beneath every revolutionary ideal, we find a conviction that man has become the tool of his tools, and that he must once more become an end and a value in himself."[14]

The widespread attention already accorded Revel's book is undoubtedly due in part to our interest as Americans to be ahead of everyone else. But we mustn't succumb to the temptation to believe that we are spearheading a revolution of worldwide significance because of some inherent superiority in us. Our affluence and our technology have probably been the primary instruments in forcing us to become individually and socially introspective (and neither the affluence nor the technology are due to a natural superiority, either).

Whatever questions can be raised about the order of Maslow's hierarchy of needs, it is clear that the satisfaction of physiological and safety needs is not enough. We have distinctive human needs of a higher order that must be satisfied. As Warren Bennis has written, "We must eternally confront and test our humanness and become more fully human."[15]

In this introspection of which I speak (a confrontation with ourselves, actually), we are beginning to look at man quite differently. He is not a tool to build better technology (as Revel insists, ". . . technological civilization [is] a means and not . . . an end"[16]). He does not exist for the organization; rather, the organization exists for him. He is not to be exploited by others for their ends; he exploits opportunities for his own sake.

One of the most striking examples of man's new view of himself lies in the changing work ethic. In the Judeo-Christian tradition, work has been presented as the punishment for Original Sin. In the human condition, work is a painful burden from which, in this world, man cannot escape.

But we are beginning to escape—not from work, but from the burden of it. It is true that work is essential to the human condition. It dignifies him, gives him pleasure and gratification. Through work man enhances himself, grows in stature, and realizes what he is capable of being—what he cannot be happy *not* being.

And much of the impetus for this perspective on man-the-worker—a fact that many commentators on our changing social scene have overlooked—comes from business corporations. That same business world that has so often been characterized (and justly) as dehumanizing, unintellectual, backward-looking, and conservative has become a leading edge in the quest for values that truly reflect the human condition and the potential of man.

Business has become a leading edge because the *need* is there—and so are the resources. Industry is facing up to certain truths:

• Most people work at dull, uninspiring jobs that are meaningless to them.

• Most people develop no more than a small fraction of their potential.

• Much of our education and training is ineffective, irrelevant, and fails to provide the growth opportunity beneficial to individuals and their organizations.

It is an expensive waste of our resources, one that we now realize we cannot longer afford.

How fast this realization is growing has been demonstrated for me by two contrasting experiences in a period of only three years. In the summer of 1968, I attended a seminar at a well-known university on "The Management of Improvement." Most of the participants were industrial engineers—specialists who have, in the past few decades, been traditionally called upon by corporations to achieve more effective operations. The attendees represented some of the largest corporations in the country, and I have no doubt that they reflected the attitudes of their employers when, in discussion after discussion, they elevated procedures, systems, and structure over people. In fact, no one there talked about *persons*. Employees were referred to as population, headcount, and census.

Three years later, many of these same corporations are sponsoring a fast-growing organization called the OD (for Organizational Development) Network. The objective of OD is not to win acceptance of people as an important asset; rather, that people *are* the business, the business organization *is* people. A new business culture is in the making, one in which:

• decisions are made by consensus to insure that everyone who has something to contribute to decision-making *does* contribute, and that everyone who has to carry out the decision is emotionally and intellectually committed to it;

• relationships between people are characterized by collaboration rather than competition, by trust rather than by suspicion, by openness rather than by compartmentalization;

• productivity is seen as a function of the integration of personal and organizational goals;

• power and authority are distributed on the basis of people's need for them and ability to exercise them rather than on the basis of executives' willingness to share them;

• no dichotomy exists between people and productivity; that is, concern for people is concern for productivity.

The focus has shifted from population to the *person*. Chris Argyris writes with profound significance, "The challenge of organizational development is close to, if not part of the very foundation for the design of a new quality of life that looks upon a man's potentiality as not only something to be revered in words but also to be continually actualized in systems that respect and require human dignity and organizational health."[17]

The focus has shifted from quantity to *quality*.

I am not so naïve as to imply that a ripple has become a tidal wave. OD—as a movement, as a philosophy—is new. Its data base is small. We have perhaps much more the desire for it, the need for it, than the scientific knowledge necessary to fulfill those needs. There is as yet more theory than empirical evidence of what will transform the organizational culture. We do not have a clear model of the organization of the future, the environment that will help us achieve the objectives we seek. OD personnel are often still found too removed from the power centers in their companies to wield the influence that is required to promote change. Corporations, to a great extent, have not yet awakened to the fact that they, rather than the universities, provide the great learning laboratories for our industrial society. We know the importance of learning, but we still do not know very much about how people learn effectively.

All of these problems legitimately generate a certain anxiety about where we are going—and how we are to get there. A few years ago, Warren Bennis wrote, "I think that the future I describe is not necessarily a 'happy' one. Coping with rapid change, living in temporary work systems, developing meaningful relations and then breaking them—all augur social strains and psychological tensions."[18]

I am inclined to believe that what Bennis describes as the future will be, for most of us, a happy one. I have no doubt that, despite the "strains" and "tensions," the workingman is bound to achieve more gratification in a corporate society that regards him as a person, values his goals, and provides nearly unlimited opportunities for him to achieve them. Only when a man is capable of realizing himself, that is to say, his potential, is there any real chance, in my opinion, that he will be happy and productive throughout his lifetime.

Furthermore, I have no doubt that the OD movement will gather force and gain acceptance. Through research, we will learn more about how people learn; we will be able to construct more effective organizational models, based on human needs; we will acquire more sophisticated skills in dealing effectively with each other as human beings.

But we cannot ignore that the revolution is already upon us. Our organizations have to be able to cope with the values of the new work force, as we discussed in Chapter Two. If our technology is not to outstrip our ability to utilize it for our own sake, we must have effective ways to train people in the problem-solving and decision-making skills that are requisite to handle it. We cannot close our eyes to the information explosion and our need to know.

We can expect more theory, more experiential learning. Undoubtedly in time we shall enjoy better tools. In the meantime, we should take advantage of what we already know, the tools that are available to us now.

The task force, as I have described it in this book, is a tool that has proved successful. We know what can be accomplished with it, even though relatively few organizations have made extensive use of it. We already know how to train people to be effective on task forces. We can recognize that the task force as a concept and as a technique goes *with* the grain of the forces of change in business. We know that widespread use of the task force can help us control, advance, and benefit from the revolution that promises to transform our society.

The future is already here. It is up to us to make it work.

REFERENCES

1. McGregor, Douglas, *The Human Side of Enterprise*. New York: McGraw-Hill Book Company, 1960, pp. 33–34.

2. Speer, Albert, *Inside the Third Reich*. New York: The Macmillan Company, 1970, pp. 286–87.

3. "Peter Drucker Attacks: Our Top-Heavy Corporations," *Dun's*, April 1971, p. 39.

4. Drucker, Peter F., *The Age of Discontinuity*. New York: Harper & Row, 1969, p. 193.

5. Argyris, Chris, *Management and Organizational Development*. New York: McGraw-Hill Book Company, 1971.

6. Bennis, Warren G., and Slater, Philip E., *The Temporary Society*. New York: Harper & Row, 1968, p. 4.

7. Jennings, E. E., *The Mobile Manager*. Ann Arbor: Bureau of Industrial Relations, University of Michigan, 1967.

8. *Dun's,* April 1971, p. 39.

9. Argyris, op. cit., p. 183.

10. McGregor, op. cit., p. 49.

11. Likert, Rensis, *The Human Organization.* New York: McGraw-Hill Book Company, 1967.

12. Drucker, op. cit., p. 55.

13. Bennis and Slater, op. cit., pp. 73–74.

14. Revel, Jean-François, *Without Marx or Jesus.* Garden City, New York: Doubleday & Company, pp. 1 and 209.

15. Bennis and Slater, op. cit., p. 125.

16. Revel, op. cit., p. 242.

17. Argyris, op. cit., p. 196.

18. Bennis and Slater, op. cit., p. 75.

RECOMMENDED READING

In addition to the above references, the following books may be helpful to those who wish more background in Organization Development, job enrichment, motivation, group dynamics, and management-by-objectives.

Blake, Robert R., and Mouton, Jane S., *Corporate Excellence Through Grid Organization Development*. Houston: Gulf Publishing Company, 1968.

Bradford, Leland P., (ed.), *Group Development* (selected readings), National Training Laboratories, 1961.

Ford, Robert N., *Motivation Through the Work Itself*. New York: American Management Association, 1969.

Fordyce, Jack K., and Weil, Raymond, *Managing with People*. Reading, Massachusetts: Addison-Wesley Publishing Company, 1971.

Foulkes, Fred, *Creating More Meaningful Work*. New York: American Management Association, 1969.

Herzberg, Frederick, *Work and the Nature of Man*. Cleveland: World Publishing Company, 1966.

Lippitt, Gordon L., *Organization Renewal*. New York: Appleton-Century-Crofts, 1969.

Maher, John R., (ed.), *New Perspectives in Job Enrichment*. New York: Van Nostrand Reinhold Company, 1971.

Maslow, A. H., *Motivation and Personality* (Second Edition). New York: Harper & Row, 1970.

Myers, M. Scott, *Every Employee a Manager*. New York: McGraw-Hill Book Company, 1970.

Odiorne, George S., *Management by Objectives*. New York: Pitman Publishing Corporation, 1965.

Reddin, W. J., *Effective Management by Objectives*. New York: McGraw-Hill Book Company, 1971.

Vroom, Victor H., *Work and Motivation*. New York: John Wiley & Sons, 1964.

Addison-Wesley Series on Organization Development, Reading, Massachusetts, 1969:

Beckhard, Richard, *Organization Development: Strategies and Models*.

Bennis, Warren G., *Organization Development: Its Nature, Origins, and Prospects*.

Blake, Robert R., and Mouton, Jane S., *Building a Dynamic Corporation Through Grid Organization Development*.

Lawrence, Paul R., and Lorsch, Jay W., *Developing Organizations: Diagnosis and Action*.

Schein, Edgar H., *Process Consultation: Its Role in Organization Development*.

Walton, Richard E., *Interpersonal Peacemaking: Confrontations and Third-Party Consultation*.

N